CONCILIUM

Religion in the Seventies

CONCILIUM

Religion in the Seventies

MAN IN A NEW SOCIETY

Edited by
Franz Böckle

Herder and Herder

1972
HERDER AND HERDER NEW YORK
232 Madison Avenue, New York 10016

1234567890   BPBP   765432

CONTENTS

PART II
BULLETINS

CONTEMPORARY AMERICAN ROMANTICISM

PART III
DOCUMENTATION CONCILIUM

Editorial

THE theologians' convention arranged by *Concilium* in Brussels in Autumn 1970 brought together a good number of contributors to our section for the first time. The plan of the present issue derives from that meeting of minds. We very soon agreed that any attempt to substantiate ethical standards for people in our society has to take into account a very much altered and diversified form of self-awareness. Some typical aspects of this new self-consciousness are described in this number, and some consideration is given to the problems which the situation poses for theological ethics. Of course the magnitude of this theme made clear from the start that the present deliberations would be more a series of indications and stimuli than a comprehensive analysis. The actual contributions bear out this prognosis.

The sociologist Wolf Lepenies introduces the debate with his very critical account of paradigms of the discussion of ethics in philosophical, biological and ethnological anthropology. He finds these part-anthropologies inadequate and therefore predicts the development of an interdisciplinary "human science". This new discipline must be oriented to the social sciences since on the one hand it is concerned with the societal determinations of its findings and on the other hand demonstrates to what extent social behaviour must also be analysed in terms of existing anthropological data. Lepenies asks theologians to join in a dialogue with sociologists in order to discuss the question of a proficient grounding of ethics. He believes that the task of theology lies not so much in the working out of a unified ethics as in the establishment of criteria for the compatibility of diverse moral systems. In this regard we may certainly say that, by the liberation of human reason within the bounds of its contingency, theology opens up the possibility of a plurality of actual expressions of morality. Nevertheless any compatibility of the various projects must be clearly distinguished from wholly arbitrary choice.

On the basis of reason grounded in faith, theology must also find expression in terms of criticism and stimulation. In so doing it must of course comply with the change in human self-understanding—as this is made apparent to theologians from without. An example of this is available in John Cobb's introduction to American "process philosophy". The Second Vatican Council (cf. Delhaye's article) realized the significance of such proposals of human self-understanding and recognized the intrinsic value of the world as a partner for theology. In this respect the New Testament shows itself to be a particularly valuable and fruitful source of reference in debate, for it offers and requires a constant human renewal which reveals and overcomes the one-sided nature of actual projects.

The contributions of Hollenweger, Astier and Cocagnac and the Bulletin tackle the question of a change of self-understanding in specific social groups. Schlette shows how the criticism emanating from certain utopian writings can contribute to a socio-critical refinement of awareness. This is all the more remarkable today, when considerable emphasis is laid (in various quarters) on the suspicion that recourse to utopia is only a shirking of responsibility for the concrete tasks of the present moment.

FRANZ BÖCKLE

PART I
ARTICLES

Wolf Lepenies

Difficulties of Basing Ethics on Anthropology

IN THE dialogue with theology sociology seems to have taken over the role of philosophy. Theology is interested in "a redefinition of the human", but can derive little help from philosophy; it is the social sciences with which theology has entered into "a dialogue about the understanding of man" and in whose "reflection on the totality of our existing social environment" it wishes to participate in order to work out "basic anthropological concepts and norms for political and ethical activity".[1] This programme is appropriate to an age in which the process of secularization has become an historical phenomenon, that is, one which can be analysed with reference to the past. The tendency to a dialogue with the social sciences thus also reflects theology's transformed, almost secularized, awareness of its role.

But if theology allows anthropology to lay down norms of ethical behaviour, we are faced with the possibility of the replacement of theology by anthropology. This is merely the consequence of the claim that any ethics is applied anthropology.[2] If

[1] H.-N. Janowski, "Theologie als kritisch orientierende Wissenschaft", in H.-G. Geyer, H.-N. Janowski, A. Schmidt, *Theologie und Soziologie* (Stuttgart, 1970), pp. 57–8.
[2] W. Trillhaas, "Spaltung und Einheit der Ethik", *Neue Zeitschrift für systematische Theologie und Religionsphilosophie* 13 (1971), p. 21. Insisting on a "theological axiomatics" in opposition to this view also presupposes a criticism of anthropological attempts to validate theological statements. Cf. G. Sauter, "Die Begründung theologischer Aussagen—wissenschaftstheoretisch gesehen", *Zeitschrift für evangelische Ethik* 15 (1971), pp. 299–308. The suggestion that reductive validation should be replaced by the

there was no such thing as philosophical anthropology before
the seventeenth century because philosophy and theology were
not yet separate, it now seems as if that separation may be on the
point of ending, since philosophy and theology, at least in their
ethical aspects, are trying to reduce themselves to anthropology.

Hans-Norbert Janowski's programme, from which I quoted
at the beginning of the article, did not mention anthropology,
but "basic anthropological concepts and norms" with which
sociology was to provide theology. Such a statement seems to me
to involve dubious assumptions about both sociology and anthropology. Fundamental is the assumption that sociology, the theory
of society, is based on anthropology, that sociological propositions can be directly related to anthropological data. The possibility of basing social theory on anthropology is, however, still
disputed;[3] or again, the ground of the argument is threatened
by the premiss that, even in the natural state, man can be understood only as a social being. As Ferguson said in his *Essay on the
History of Civil Society* (1767), among men society appears to be
as old as the individual, and the use of language as general as
that of hand or foot. Social theory must "abandon the assumption that society 'consists' of men"—since it is this assumption
which makes social *theory* possible in the first place.[4]

A similar development can be seen in anthropology—the growing tendency to "sociologization". Its full extent can be appreci-
ated only when one stops thinking of "anthropology" as a single
academic discipline. In German the term would imply physical
or philosophical anthropology, in French a combination of physical anthropology and ethnology, in England "social anthropology" and in the U.S.A. "anthropology" in the sense of
ethnology. On the other hand, it seems more useful to separate

---

criterion of the duty to communicate, and theological concepts understood
as "regulators of church language", there is a similarity to the views of
Jürgen Habermas. Cf. J. Habermas and N. Luhmann, *Theorie des Gesellschaft oder Sozialtechnologie—was leistet die Systemforschung?* (Frankfurt a.M., 1971).

[3] Cf. W. Lepenies and H. Nolte, *Kritik der Anthropologie* (Munich,
1971).

[4] N. Luhmann, "Systemtheoretische Argumentationen. Eine Entgegnung
auf Jürgen Habermas", Habermas and Luhmann, *Theorie der Gesellschaft
oder Sozialtechnologie, op. cit.*, p. 385.

biological (physical), ethnological and philosophical anthropology, and to use the term "anthropology" for the whole range of anthropological disciplines. If in these terms we consider the current state of research in the three "subsidiary disciplines", the impression of an interdisciplinary convergence seems to me unmistakable. In addition, the anthropological disciplines are becoming more conscious than ever before of the extent to which their statements are determined by society and have an effect upon it. This awareness takes different forms in the different disciplines, but there exists sufficient common ground to allow us to speak of "sociological anthropology".[5]

An important factor contributing to this is that attempts to relate anthropological questions to Marxist thought now provoke much less opposition than, for example, in the 1950s. In reaction to attempts to emphasize Marx's early writings, with their more anthropological orientation, at the expense of the political and economic analyses of the later Marx, any attempts to work out a Marxist anthropology were suppressed in the Socialist countries. Now, with the tendency swinging more towards an integration of Marx's early works into the totality of his writings, it is possible to consider a Marxist anthropology more impartially. Outlines of Marxist theories of personality inspired even by Communist Parties are being published, and the many attempts to develop a "socialist ethics" are also part of this newly acquired freedom with regard to anthropological problems.[6]

The "sociologization" of anthropology thus justifies the suggestion that theology should turn to anthropology for an answer to its questions about the possibility of finding a basis for moral principles outside theology. Such a dialogue becomes even more valuable when we see that in the anthropological disciplines themselves reflection on their social basis has been stimulated or even started by a debate on the problem of ethics. In what follows I wish to offer a critical description of paradigms of the discus-

[5] Cf. W. Lepenies, *Soziologische Anthropologie. Materialien* (Munich, 1971).

[6] Against this, for the most thoroughgoing attempt to date to relegate attempts to construct an anthropology from Marx's work to the realm of ideology, cf. L. Althusser, *For Marx* (London and New York, 1970); L. Althusser and N. Balibar, *Reading Capital* (London and New York, 1971; an abridged version of *Lire le Capital*, 2 vols., Paris, 1968).

sion about ethics in philosophical, biological and ethnological anthropology. I hope that this will show that the difficulties connected with the discussion of ethical questions point, in all the disciplines, to the primacy of social theory in finding a basis for norms. I cannot reconstruct the history of ethical questions in anthropology, but I shall simply mention the originators of particular lines of argument at various points of the discussion.

I. ETHICS IN PHILOSOPHICAL ANTHROPOLOGY

Reflections on the connection between ethics and anthropology, and more specifically about the possibility of an anthropological basis for ethical propositions, turn out to be predominantly questions for *philosophical anthropology*. In this sense, the history of philosophical anthropology is also a history of ethics, and there is theoretical significance in the fact that Max Scheler, whose book *Man's Place in the Cosmos* (1928) had such a marked influence on philosophical anthropology, attempted to outline an ethics of values. The most impressive example of the intertwining of philosophical anthropology and ethics, however, is to be found in Arnold Gehlen's work, in which revisions of anthropological questions result directly in a different view of ethics.

Gehlen's importance still rests on his construction of a conservative anthropology. The essence of this can be found in his major work, *Der Mensch* (1940): it is not instincts which adapt men to institutions, but rather the plasticity and instability of the structure of human impulses which requires a stabilizing institutional support. Gehlen's frightening picture of the "terrible" state of man in nature is not the result of a fear of man's instincts or residual instincts as such but of the results of the release of instincts. Any *behaviour analogous to instinct*, all expressions of the *second nature*, such as "the accomplishments of jugglers and acrobats, who . . . as it were cultivate intelligence in their limbs" ("Reflexionen über Gewohnheit" (1927), in the Driesch Festschrift), win his explicit admiration.

In *Der Mensch*, Gehlen calls the institutions which replace instincts the "highest control systems"; they set standards for human behaviour. It can now be seen why this outline of anthropology can do without a proficient ethics; it is already complete in its theory of institutions and its concept of man as a creature of "discipline". *Morality* is a crucial term in his position, and Gehlen calls it "a biological necessity present in man alone"— but none the less it has no biological *basis*: "We do not act in this or that way because we have particular needs, but we have those needs because we ourselves and the people around us act in this or that way."[7] The existence of norms of human behaviour is thus the result of *biological* forces, but *culturally* determined— anthropology and the theory of institutions fit so tightly together than there is no room left for ethics. Basing ethics on the force of instincts is totally impossible. There is no escape from the dilemma between compiling an arbitrary but comprehensive catalogue of instincts for man in general and having a conception of a particular man in terms of instincts. In the one case ethics becomes arbitrary and so useless in particular cases, in the other it only works for the individual and so loses any applicability to society.

The affinity between anthropology and institutional theory which makes ethics superfluous becomes very clear in the chapter of Gehlen's major work entitled "Character", because "character" does not occur as an anthropological term. In a review of Herder's *Ideas on the Philosophy of Human History*, Kant suggested an anthropology which would not "stumble in the footprints of physiology or fly on the wings of metaphysics", but would be based on the *actions* of men, "by which they reveal their character".[8] And John Stuart Mill defined ethnology, the science of human nature as he called it, as the science of the formation of character.[9] In the tradition of philosophical anthropology the idea of character denotes the border at which the connection between anthropological basis and institutional superstructure can be revealed. It can be seen here, too, that ethics must remain redundant in the context of Gehlen's original anthropology: the dominant habits of action—which is how Gehlen defines "character"—rests on acquired instincts, i.e., they are not determined by nature. Character is rather "the product of train-

---

[7] A. Gehlen, *Der Mensch. Seine Natur und seine Stellung in der Welt* (Frankfurt–Bonn, [8]1966), p. 330.

[8] Kant, *Werke*, vol. 10 (Darmstadt, [2]1964), pp. 793–5.

[9] John Stuart Mill, *A System of Logic* (London, 1843).

ing in the society in which it lives and society's order of priorities". In contrast, any ethics ought to be concerned with the possibilities of transcendence contained in the moral systems of specific societies.

In *Moral und Hypermoral* (1969) Gehlen revised his original anthropology. I cannot discuss in detail the contradictions of this version—it has been criticized by Jürgen Habermas and Helmuth Plessner.[10] In this book he offers an account of ethics, and this itself is enough to confirm the view that he has altered his own anthropology—even if he himself would reject the charge. If we recall the original interlacing of anthropology and institutional theory, and its systematic basis, this complementary relation cannot remain unaffected by an account of ethics. The conclusion is inevitable: ethics now has to provide what institutional theory can no longer take for granted: binding rules for behaviour. In *Moral und Hypermoral*, however, Gehlen does not so much reveal the connection between man's openness to the world, the weakness of institutional guarantees and an ethics which makes up for this weakness, but rather offers the paradox of an ethical programme based on biological determinism.

The original interlacing of anthropology and institutional theory holds, with the result that the replacement of the latter by ethics cannot but affect the catalogue of basic anthropological concepts: in contrast to his earlier views, Gehlen now sees man more as a creature controlled by instincts. But someone so sure of the anthropological premises which leave their marks on behaviour and give institutions their solidity ought not to need the postulate of ethics. Poised uneasily on the new, more strongly instinct-dominated anthropology, ethics is additional to biological determinism, and points either to the fragility of the premisses

[10] A. Gehlen, *Moral und Hypermoral. Eine pluralistische Ethik* (Frankfurt–Bonn, 1969). Criticisms of this include J. Habermas, "Nachgeahmte Substantialität. Eine Auseinandersetzung mit Arnold Gehlens Ethik", *Merkur* 264 (1970), pp. 313–27, and H. Plessner, "Trieb und Ethik", *Merkur* 276 (1971), pp. 307–15. Cf. W. Lepenies, "Anthropologie und Gesellschaftskritik. Zur Kontroverse Gehlen–Habermas", in Lepenies and Nolte, *Kritik der Anthropologie, op. cit.*, pp. 77–102. This essay also appeared in *Soziologen-Korrespondenz* 4 (1970), pp. 171–98, and in both a French and English translation in *The Human Context* 3 (1971), pp. 205–25, 226–48.

or to the author's unease—or perhaps to both. "Ethics" has moved from institution theory to anthropology—though an anthropology which had no need of an ethical superstructure. Nothing sums up this situation better than Gehlen's concept of "physiological virtues". What is the point of ethics if physiology already guarantees virtue?

Gehlen's "new anthropology", in my view, can be interpreted as a reaction to a political, but not just political, movement which no longer restricts itself to making institutions "insecure" but wants to experiment with the very basis of human nature—among other ways by spreading the "new morality". Since such a position can no longer be met with an anthropology which starts from the release of man's instincts and the plasticity of his impulses, *anthropology becomes rigid and ethics anthropological.*

At the same time, however, Gehlen's account of ethics runs into the same difficulties as any other attempt to derive ethics ultimately from ethological assumptions. If catalogues of social norms are referred back to the anthropologically based norms of human behaviour, ethics appears superfluous because physiology already contains virtue. But if it is the function of ethics to counteract the absence of virtue in man's natural state, that is, to be an anti-anthropology, it can only be put into effect by *force.* The question then arises whether we can still speak of ethics when "moral" principles have to be imposed by forces.[11] Once upon a time Gehlen would have been able to avoid the dilemma because his institutional theory occupied the place of ethics. Now that ethics has retrieved its place, human nature becomes both the "terrible state of nature" and the basis of virtue at the same time. But ethics cannot be derived from an arbitrary anthropology.

[11] This seems to be no problem for Gehlen: "A science whose aim was to describe the various forms of ethos would be called 'ethics', and should be the first to realize that a total dominant ethos, i.e., one which relativizes, subordinates or excludes other forms, does not come into existence without a dominant class which proclaims and imposes its ethos", *Moral und Hypermoral, op. cit.,* p. 38. This makes it clear that while pluralism in ethics is theoretically possible in Gehlen's view, in practice an ethical system can only be imposed by force.

II. Ethics in Biological Anthropology

If I now turn to questions of biological anthropology, I shall be making a distinction between ethological and biological attempts to find a basis for ethical principles. Some comparative psychologists (ethologists) attempt to draw conclusions about human ethics from forms of animal behaviour analogous to morality and to trace the roots of human ethics in the history of the species.[12] Just as theology in its dialogue with sociology seems to distance itself from philosophy, so ethology, in putting itself forward as the basis of ethics or moral theology, seems to be trying to outdo sociology. A "biology of the ten commandments" in practice acknowledges social theory only as a special case of the study of behaviour in general; it makes sociology an auxiliary discipline to ethology. This programme had its historical prototypes in the eighteenth and nineteenth centuries; an attempt to revive it would mean once more challenging sociology's claim to be an autonomous discipline. The reactions to the claim of ethology to be a complete science of behaviour (including sociology) have been correspondingly sharp, even if not always securely based methodologically.[13]

The increased importance of ethology can be seen in philosophical anthropology. Arnold Gehlen originally based his anthropology on a "rejection of instinct theories"; now he stresses the "very high biological content of anthropological problems" and lays emphasis on their "common ground with the physiology of behaviour". I have already briefly discussed the reasons for this shift of interest.

In their search for the instinctual basis of human behaviour, ethologists think they can demonstrate "the biological basis for ethical norms" (Eibl-Eibesfeldt), "forms of animal behaviour analogous to morality" (Lorenz) and even a "biology of the ten commandments" (Wickler). Eibl-Eibesfeldt maintains that "aggressive and altruistic behaviour are both programmed in advance

[12] Cf. I. Eibl-Eibesfeldt, *Grundriss der vergleichenden Verhaltensforschung. Ethologie* (Munich, 1967); *Liebe und Hass. Zur Naturgeschichte elementarer Verhaltensweisen* (Munich, 1970). K. Lorenz, *On Aggression* (London, 1966); W. Wickler, *Antworten der Verhaltensforschung* (Munich, 1970); *Die Biologie der zehn Gebote* (Munich, 1971).

[13] Cf. H. Arendt, *On Violence* (London and New York, 1970).

by adaptations which took place during the history of the species, and that there are therefore predetermined norms for our ethical behaviour. Man's aggressive impulses are counterbalanced by ... equally deep-rooted tendencies to sociability and mutual assistance."[14] This statement of principle shows the difficulty of finding a basis for ethics in ethology. If aggression and altruism are both programmed in advance by the history of the species, it is equally possible to justify aggressive and altruistic actions. But norms for social behaviour cannot be derived from or justified by such origins in the history of the species; the fact of a conflict of norms in biology also points rather to the necessity of finding a basis for ethics by some means other than ethological reduction. Kant had already seen this clearly when he recognized "antagonism", man's unsociable sociability, as the mainspring of human evolution, but at the same time saw that the solution to the problems it caused was no longer to be found set out in nature, but only in "a civil society which will generally administer justice" (*Idee zu einer allgemeinen Geschichte in weltbürgerlicher Absicht*, 1784). The result of this awareness on subsequent work was the abandonment of physiological or metaphysical guidelines in anthropology—it seemed rather that it needed to be supplemented by legal and social theory.

Ethologists such as Eibl-Eibesfeldt themselves admit functional conflicts between different norms and the inevitable historical relativity of any attempt to find a basis for norms, but they do not draw the logical conclusion and give up the attempt to find a biological foundation for ethical principles. "The discovery that a tendency is hereditary in us is not sufficient to justify it", as Eibl-Eibesfeldt says, and it also makes attempts to find a biological basis for social norms redundant. The system of human impulses is "value-free", but if one examines the behaviour of adults one "is constantly involved in value judgments". If this situation is described as a "disturbance"[15] of the learning process of natural science, the dilemma of any attempt to base ethics on ethology becomes apparent: ethology cannot validate values by biological arguments, but it can be ethics only if it allows itself to be involved in problems of values.

[14] Eibl-Eibesfeldt, *Liebe und Hass, op. cit.*, p. 15.
[15] Wickler, *Antworten der Verhaltensforschung, op. cit.*, pp. 181, 188.

Ethology attempted to provide a foundation for norms indirectly, through a comparison with animals. This method has a long tradition, and the circumstances of its application may also be of interest to political historians. On 28 October 1794, five years after the outbreak of the French Revolution, the Convention voted to establish the Ecole Normale. According to reports in the Convention's *Journal*, in the early period of this élitist school the eighty-year-old Daubenton achieved a brilliant success as a teacher. A pupil and colleague of the great Buffon, he nevertheless ventured to criticize his master for the statement, "The lion is the king of beasts". The lion, according to Daubenton, was not a king because all the beasts fled from him and none flattered him; there was no king in nature, he said. The *Journal* reports the wild applause with which the students greeted these words, and comments: "This was the voice of public opinion, in all its purity and power, in the seat of learning. Never before had there been a clearer demonstration of hatred for the monarchy and love for the Republic."[16]

The illustration of forms of behaviour analogous to morality, which ethology tries to discover in animals, has scarcely more value for the analysis of social activity than Buffon's metaphor and Daubenton's criticism of it. The fact that a man of rage bares his teeth as a result of an inherited instinct to threaten to bite neither explains this reaction nor gives any advice on checking it. Questions about whether "a native of Papua, a Bantu, an Italian or a Japanese stamps his foot" (Eibl-Eibesfeldt) make very little contribution to our understanding of social phenomena, particularly in the wider field of sociology and economics. Man is in short, a man under any circumstances and we can learn nothing about his nature from analogies with other animals (Ferguson).

Nevertheless, the investigations and findings of ethology have an importance for sociology, not indeed because they reveal a continuity between animal and human behaviour, but because they direct our attention to what is specific in human actions. Physiological mechanisms may force animals into "selfless be-

---

[16] Cf. J. Fayet, *La révolution française et la science 1789–1795* (Paris, 1960), p. 347.

haviour directed to the welfare of the community", but neither the moral law in us nor the normative influence of social relations can be explained by analogy with such mechanisms, and the concept of "physiological virtues" is at best a piece of heuristically valuable anthropomorphism. Of course, scepticism is not justified merely with regard to attempts to give a naturalistic interpretation of the legitimation of norms; utopian views which see man as a creature freed from nature also deserve criticism. The fact that both aggression and altruism have a basis in species history does not provide a foundation for human morality, but, for example, its indication of evolutionary factors which may influence aggressive tendencies does make it easier to understand the difficulties which may stand in the way of the development of an altruistic morality. In this sense, ethology performs a useful function for ethics: it does not provide a foundation for forms of moral behaviour, but it does tell us what "natural" difficulties prevent us from putting them into practice.

An ethology which does not accept this restriction of its claim to knowledge is forgetting a part of its own "tradition". John Stuart Mill called ethology the exact science of human nature. By this he meant mainly an analysis of the laws of character formation, and I have already made the point that the concept of character points to a field which we would consider as part of anthropology. This ethology does not, in spite of the definition just mentioned, go back to the basic laws of human nature; its value lies rather—and it is close to sociology in this—in "elucidating the distinguishing features which belong to each type of particular situation and justifying the reservation of the title 'hereditary factors' only to the remainder, if there is a remainder".[17] This programme provides a division between the fields of sociology and anthropology which could help the construction of a human ethics.

In 1846 Kierkegaard expressed (in his *Journal*) the fear that physics would one day supplant ethics, just as metaphysics had supplanted theology. Today, however, physical scientists provide various forms of stimulus for a re-definition of ethics. The problems raised by such an ethics, not so much based on natural

[17] John Stuart Mill, *op. cit.*

science as postulated by scientists, can be seen clearly in the writings of the winner of the Nobel Prize for Physiology and Medicine, Jacques Monod (who won the prize in 1965 together with André Lwoff and François Jacob).[18]

In view of Monod's understanding of biology, his position can be treated completely within the limits of anthropological attempts to provide a basis for ethics, even though, as we shall show, Monod himself rejects the possibility of a scientific basis of ethics. In Monod's view, biology is concerned with problems which must be solved if we are to be able to discuss the problem of "human nature" at all in any other than metaphysical concepts. The biology based on the theory of genetic codes forms the basis of a general theory of living systems of which anthropology constitutes a special case.

Monod postulates a "choice" of an "ethics of objective knowledge" as the conclusion of a particular combination of statements from genetics and evolutionary theory.[19] In molecular biology—which can be characterized by the "application of physical methods to... biological phenomena in an attempt to interpret them by means of an investigation of molecular structures and molecular interaction"—it is regarded as proved that the reproductive mechanism of DNA (dioxyribonucleic acid), "a constituent of chromosomes, the bearer of the genotype and the basis of evolution", is responsible for the retention of deviations in the course of the evolutionary process. At the start of life processes, structures came into being by chance and were then "retained". It follows from this that a form of evolution which

---

[18] J. Monod, "Von der Molekularbiologie zur Ethik der Erkenntnis" (Inaugural lecture at the Collège de France, 3 November 1967), *The Human Context* 1 (1969), pp. 341–6; *Le hasard et la nécessité. Essai sur la philosophie naturelle de la biologie moderne* (Paris, 1970); "On the logical relationship between knowledge and values", Watson Fuller (ed.), in *The Social Impact of Modern Biology* (London, 1971), pp. 11–21; "Die Wissenschaft, der höchste Wert des Menschen", *The Human Context* 3 (1971). I shall be concerned with the publications of Monod mentioned above and shall no longer give references for individual quotations. Cf. the critical appreciation of Monod by Jean Piaget, "Hasard et dialectique en epistémologie biologique", *Sciences. Revue de la civilisation scientifique* 71 (1971), pp. 29–36.

[19] On this cf. W. Zimmermann, *Evolution und Naturphilosophie* (Berlin, 1968), pp. 239–78: "Evolution und Ethik".

depends on such randomly occurring, non-lethal deviations can no longer be based on any idea of finality—a concept which is replaced by the anti-metaphysical term "teleonomy". The findings of molecular biology imply, rather, that metaphysical theories about the origin of life on earth must be decisively rejected. From this Monod draws the conclusion that it is no longer possible to base ethics on (natural) science: "By definition, objective science knows no values. It cannot know them. It follows that it also cannot validate ethics. There is therefore no such thing as objective ethics; it is as impossible as objective morals."

On the other hand Monod insists on the necessity for a human ethics. Since this cannot be *proved*, it must be *chosen*. The choice, however, cannot be made according to individual decision, but must be directed by the criterion of productivity: since science has brought the greatest progress to mankind, the choice can only fall on an ethics of objective knowledge. Science does not provide the basis for ethics, but an ethics of objective knowledge is a basic axiom for it. This "choice" of an ethics of objective knowledge involves several problems: its internal contradictions derive ultimately from the fact that, for Monod, science, philosophy and philosophical practice are completely separate.[20]

Since Monod totally refuses to offer a basis for ethical forms of behaviour, but only postulates the choice of a particular ethics, his preference cannot be adequately criticized with logical arguments—such as, for example, by showing that the role of the utility principle in this choice produces a basis of ethics which involves values. We may still, however, criticize the optimistic view of science which, ultimately, lies behind Monod's "ethics".

[20] Cf. P. Boiteau, "Une éthique délibérément idéaliste, celle de J. Monod", *La Pensée* 155 (1971), pp. 55–77. Monod could also be criticized for failing to consider an institutional takeover of his "éthique de la connaissance", which would be only too easy. Monod approaches J. Bronowski's position. Bronowski was vehemently in favour of the "disestablishment of science". For a criticism of this concept, which is based on a utopian confidence in the ethics of scientists, see the views of Peter Medawar, Gerald Piel, Anthony Wedgwood Benn and Eugene Rabinowitch in *Encounter* 37 (1971), No. 3, pp. 91–5. It should be noted that these arguments and counter-arguments are all put forward in the context of a debate about the "free-floating intelligence" of Mannheim's sociology of knowledge.

But the dilemma of scientific ethics does not lie in the fact that science has not hitherto followed an ethics of objective knowledge, but can be seen from a consideration of the difficulties of such an ethics (the problems of progress). Monod is able to cling to the idea of the uniformity and universality of the ethics of objective knowledge only because he almost completely ignores the ambiguity of the scientific process itself. An awareness of this ambiguity would have forced Monod, who invokes Descartes in another context, to consider whether a provisional morality (*morale par provision*) as put forward in the *Discourse on Method* would not have been a more appropriate conclusion from his arguments from molecular biology.

Monod's inability to follow his arguments to this conclusion is the result, I suspect, of problems of legitimation. Monod could not retain the idea of a validation of ethics by means of (natural) science without adopting a critical attitude towards principles of "objective science" itself. His scientific ethics therefore rests on an act of non-scientific behaviour: "choice". The *scientist*'s actions may be value-free, but as a *man* he decides in favour of the value of objective knowledge. The proof of the impossibility of basing ethics on scientific assumptions is thus based in the last resort on a form of anthropology: that of the type of man whose choice as it were "naturally" falls on objective knowledge. The position of *Le hasard et la nécessité* is therefore consistent when it maintains that the ethics of objective knowledge includes a knowledge of ethics in the sense of an awareness of the possibilities and limitations of biological existence.

III. Ethics in Ethnological Anthropology

I use the phrase "ethnological anthropology" as an inclusive term for ethnology, cultural anthropology and social anthropology,[21] but shall be concerned in what follows almost exclusively with the problems of American ethnology (anthropology). The importance of ethnological anthropology in determining ethical principles is made clear by a comparison with the aims of biological anthropology. Biological anthropology tries to ex-

[21] Cf. W. Lepenies, *Soziologische Anthropologie, op. cit.*, pp. 42–76.

plain human activity, and looks for universals in human nature. The postulate that "ethics, by its very nature, is the same for all men" (Trillhaas) corresponds to this interest. In contrast to this, ethnological anthropology points to the variety of human *cultures* and the resulting diversity of human value systems. The difference in the interests of the two disciplines has been given institutional form for some time now, particularly in the U.S.A., in the division between departments of "physical" and "cultural" anthropology.

On the other hand, there is today an interdisciplinary trend in anthropological disciplines which is bringing biological and cultural anthropology together again. In practice it was impossible to associate the postulate of the unity of human nature solely with biological anthropology and the postulate of its diversity solely with ethnological anthropology. The philosophy of the Enlightenment in its day tried to establish diversity as a principle of nature, and thus justified dissimilarity and tolerated difference.

The antinomies of the anthropology of the Enlightenment can best be seen in the changing attitude to primitive and savage peoples. Whereas in the earliest accounts of travel the term "primitive" is used pejoratively, contempt for the primitive gradually gives rise to the legend of the "noble savage". It should be added that the origin of this legend is less a sign of sympathy or respect than of pressures which meant that the only way of criticizing existing conditions in one's own society was to project the criticism on to exotic societies. Similarly, the polemics against slavery in the eighteenth century were only partly the result of "humanitarian" feeling; economic considerations were equally important, as in the case of Dupont de Nemours, who argued that slaves had insufficient motivation for achievement.

The anthropology of the Enlightenment thus made a definite contribution to the weakening of ethnocentrism—but did not remove its basis. A concentration on races can still be seen in writings of the Enlightenment which today have a progressive air, such as Condorcet's *Esquisse d'un tableau historique des progrès de l'esprit humain.*[22] The contradictions of the anthropology

[22] *Op. cit.,* pp. 84–90.

of the Enlightenment are no less apparent today—the problems caused by the Europe-centred theories of civilization which dominate ethnology and the sociology of development are only one example.[23]

Equally characteristic of the antinomies of ethnological anthropology is the debate about relativism. *Cultural* relativism is a result of the discovery of the diversity of human nature. It could only become a scientific attitude, however, when the "shock" of the diversity discovered in human characteristics had been overcome (terms such as "foreign", "alien", "curiosity", "monstrosity", which strictly refer to something non-human, indicate the obstacles to this recognition) through a realization of the coherence of the foreign culture, a recognition that a system of differences was involved. In this phase the doctrine of cultural relativism, which was used as a weapon against ethnocentrism, was strongly inspired by the Enlightenment.[24]

The antithesis of relativism is universalism. This means not simply an appeal to biological constants, but the reduction of forms of social behaviour to biological causes in order to legitimate norms. Attempts have been made, for example, to justify particular aesthetic attitudes by the claim that habits of sight and the possibilities of sense perception have not changed while man has lived on earth. Relativism, on the other hand, will try to show that such attitudes are specific to a culture or class; it cannot admit the idea of a universal ethics.

It is becoming clear that—in spite of its progressive intentions —the doctrine of cultural relativism cannot provide the basis for a progressive social theory or practical social criticism. Lévi-Strauss has described this difficulty as the ethnographer's dilemma: "If he wishes to contribute to the improvement of his own social system he cannot but condemn, wherever he comes upon them, conditions analogous to those he deplores at home. He loses, in so doing, all claim to be objective and impartial. Con-

[23] Cf. D. Ribeire, *The Civilisational Process* (Washington, D.C., 1968).
[24] Cultural relativism was for a long time, and is still to a great extent today, the dominant "ethical" doctrine of ethnology. In 1948 the Executive Board of the American Anthropological Association drew up a "Statement on Human Rights" which was submitted to the U.N. The Declaration on Human Rights adopted by the U.N. General Assembly on 10 December 1949 did not, however, adopt these proposals.

versely, the detachment enjoined on him by moral scruples, and by the rigorous methods of science, will prevent him from finding fault with his own society, once it is taken for granted that his business is to know, not to pass judgment. The man who takes action in his own country cannot hope to understand the world outside: the man who takes all knowledge for his ambition must give up the idea of ever changing anything at home."[25]

In the interests of research, an attempt has been made to get over the difference between universalism and relativism by distinguishing between biological and trans-cultural constants. Precisely the same material may be involved; only the methods by which the constant features in a characteristic is discovered are different. In the first case the constant elements are found by means of the methods of natural science, while in the second they are assumed with more or less probability on the basis of a more or less comprehensive comparison of cultures. The value of the proofs in each approach is admittedly not identical, and generally the writings of conservative anthropology rely on what are claimed as "biological constants". The problems of relativism and universalism are not ultimately removed by the distinction between biological and trans-cultural constants.

Anthropological relativism suffers from the legitimation deficit of any relative discipline: it cannot validate itself, but on theoretical grounds neither can it rely on external legitimation. Anthropological relativism can only support accounts of particular systems of morality. On the other hand, if universalism attempts to describe a universal moral code it runs into the same difficulties which face the attempt to provide a biological basis for ethical principles. In the U.S.A., not least as a result of the use of ethnology in the service of imperialism, this dilemma has provoked a passionate debate on the principles of anthropological (ethnological) ethics.[26] This means more than "just" the working out of a code of conduct for anthropologists; the basic epistemological problems of the debates in the social sciences on value judgments are now gradually beginning to be discussed.

[25] Claude Lévi-Strauss, *A World on the Wane* (London 1961), p. 384.
[26] "Towards an Ethics for Anthropologists", *Current Anthropology* 12 (1971), pp. 321–56.

IV. Anthropology, Sociology, Theology

Schopenhauer said, "Preaching morality is easy; justifying it is difficult." This is clear, too, from the attempts to validate ethics by means of anthropology. The problem has lost none of its urgency, since ultimately, according to Roger Bastide, the debate on value judgments can make very little progress until the foundations of a scientific morality are laid.[27] If the belief still exists in the anthropological disciplines that ethical principles can be validated by reference to human nature, not only can this be criticized for clinging to an unhistorical anthropology,[28] but its ignorance of the history of the problem is also remarkable. The antinomies of bourgeois natural law appear unchanged. In Hobbes the laws of nature are in direct conflict with natural instincts (*Leviathan* XVII); *norms*, which are essential to the functioning of social life, cannot be derived from the *rules* of natural processes.[29] Pierre Bayle had an answer to the question about the voice of nature in 1704: it says "that we must eat and drink. If we did not correct nature, there would be nothing more corrupt than the human soul."

That "ethics by its very nature is the same for all men" (Trillhaas) follows logically from the assumption that ethics can in fact be derived from human nature in general. Without wishing to reject this possibility finally, we may note that a realization of the difficulties of validating ethics by anthropology indicates at least the variability of human nature, even in primary needs: "Hunger is hunger, but hunger which satisfies itself with cooked meat eaten with a knife and fork is a different kind of hunger

---

[27] Cf. R. Bastide, *Anthropologie Appliquée* (Paris, 1971), p. 39.

[28] This position has been overtaken even within the anthropological sciences; in this connection I am thinking particularly of research which shows the historical change and "spatial" differentiation of structures of needs. In connection with the programme of an "historical anthropology" I have given references in my previously mentioned book *Soziologische Anthropologie* to publications by R. Koselleck, Th. Nipperdey and H. U. Wehler. Cf. W. Lepenies, *op. cit.*, pp. 38–41.

[29] F. Borkenau, *Der übergang vom feudalen zum bürgerlichen Weltbild. Studien zur Geschichte der Philosophie der Manufakturperiode* (Paris, 1934), photographic reproduction Darmstadt, 1971, pp. 439–82 ("Hobbes").

from that which devours raw flesh with hands, nails and teeth."[30]

The realization of the variability of human nature which theology acquires from its dialogue with anthropology makes an analysis of the particularity of human norms an urgent matter. Since very different systems of norms can perform the same functions, the fact of this functional equivalence directs theology also to sociology. The "highest moral principles give us no information about what the morality of a particular society really is, but about what the moralist in each case imagines the morality to be".[31] And the consequence of the difficulties involved in basing a universal ethics on anthropology, which ultimately means a return to the idea of natural law, is today the attempt "to provide a substitute for what 'nature' was in natural law" (Luhmann).

The suggestion that, in order to tackle the problem of validating ethics, theology should first begin a dialogue with sociology gives a high priority to the problem of the empirical finding of a multiplicity of norms.[32] It is not in practice within the power of sociology to investigate why members of different classes in the same society or members of different societies should observe differing moral principles when the different systems of norms have equivalent functions. This view is completely intelligible in terms of a critical theory of society: unified moral systems, particularly when they claim an anthropological basis, are generally the expression of variable norms within a society and widely differing sanctions between different strata of the society. This

[30] K. Marx, *Grundrisse der Kritik der politischen ökonomie* (Berlin, GDR, 1953), p. 13.

[31] N. Luhmann, "Normen in soziologischer Perspektive", *Soziale Welt* 20 (1969), p. 29.

[32] Little insight is needed to anticipate defensive reactions to such a suggestion. In a review of Peter Berger's book, *Invitation to Sociology. A Humanistic Perspective*—the argument of which I do not intend to reproduce—we read: "We [ancient historians and Latinists] will only accept the invitation if sociology makes up its mind to become a discipline of history, philosophy and ethics. Otherwise ... [we] will expel it from the *Universitas litterarum*, for not only does it represent 'the consciousness of a world whose value concepts have been made relative by the bank', but it provides this consciousness with a theory, if it has not in many cases itself produced the consciousness; it is the forerunner of the decline of the West, of the twilight of the gods." H. Drexler, "Einladung zur Soziologie", *Zeitschrift für Religions- und Geistesgeschichte* 23 (1971), pp. 147-55.

does not mean that anthropological investigation has become obsolete; it remains an essential complement to that of sociology. Ethnological anthropology makes it easier to change norms by its discovery of the multiplicity of norm systems and prevents the construction of ethnocentric catalogues of norms. Biological anthropology can indicate not just the *limits* of man but the variety of human *possibilities*; ethology took up a position in just this way with its criticism of the Church's sexual morality.[33]

This approach admittedly does not remove the difficulties produced by a relativism with regard to norm systems—for example, functional equivalence does not prevent clashes between moral systems. In fact one possible task of theology may lie in this area: not so much to set its sights on working out a uniform ethical system, as to work out criteria for the *compatibility* of different systems of morality. This is a task for the present. If mankind, in fact, grows into a "world society",[34] working out a unified ethics may once more become urgent. But perhaps a world society can only function and avoid stagnation if it has a number of clearly distinct but mutually compatible moral systems.

Translated by Francis McDonagh

[33] Cf. W. Wickler, "Das Missverstandnis des ehelichen Aktes in der Moraltheologie", *Antworten der Verhaltensforschung, op. cit.*, pp. 195–220.
[34] On the interpretation of this concept in system theory cf. N. Luhmann, "Die Weltgesellschaft", *Archiv für Rechts- und Sozialphilosophie* 57 (1971), pp. 1–35.

John Cobb

Man in Process

PROCESS philosophy in the broadest sense includes all modes of
thought that see event, change, or becoming as more fundamental categories for the understanding of the world than substance and being. Heraclitus and Protagoras are early examples
of process thinking in the West, and Buddhist philosophy provides clear examples in the East. In modern times Hume and
Hegel have set the stage for very influential and very divergent
forms of process philosophy. Evolutionary theory in biology and
the breakdown of the Newtonian world view of classical mech-
anics have given fresh impetus to process thinking in this century. Bergson and Teilhard in France, and James and Dewey
in the United States, come to mind. Heidegger and Sartre can
also be claimed as process thinkers in so far as their analysis of
human existence is concerned.

In the United States at the present time, however, process
philosophy has come to have a narrower meaning. While claim-
ing kinship and indebtedness to many of the men mentioned
above, it has come under the dominant influence of Alfred North
Whitehead. Since generalizations about the view of man in all
forms of process thinking would remain extremely abstract, this
essay will deal with the implications of Whitehead's philosophy
for man's understanding of himself. The first section emphasizes
features of his thought shared with many other process philosophers. The second section deals with more distinctive doctrines.
The third section considers implications or developments of his
thought of special importance for theology.

Whitehead was an Englishman who devoted most of his life
to mathematics, logic and the philosophy of nature. He is recognized as having made important contributions in those fields,
but he belongs more to the history of their development than to
the present discussion. Late in life he accepted a call to a chair
in philosophy at Harvard University, and in the 1920s and 1930s
he wrote a series of books in which he developed an intricate
and comprehensive ontological and cosmological vision. The
most important and also the most difficult of these books is
Process and Reality. Because Whitehead's ideas were difficult
and philosophical attention was turned away from ontological
and cosmological questions, Whitehead's speculative writings
had little influence throughout the 1940s. In the 1950s, however, his following grew in size and enthusiasm, and in the
1960s a much clearer and more widespread understanding of
his work has established him as a major influence in American
thought.

I

First, in common with much other process thought, Whitehead sees man as an emergent within nature. Scientifically this
view is hardly disputable today, but it is far from commanding
serious assent among all philosophers and theologians. On the
contrary, it cuts sharply against all those traditions that have
been shaped by an epistemological starting-point. They begin in
and with human experience, as understood either by the British
empiricists or by the Continental idealists and phenomenologists.
In that context they ask what the natural or non-human world
can be known to be. The world is then seen as the humanly
experienced world. In the extreme, but not uncommon, case the
world is treated as a function of human consciousness. That consciousness cannot then seriously regard itself as an emergent
within that world.

Whitehead holds that philosophy should follow science and
recognize the place of conscious human experience in the process
of evolutionary development. He therefore affirms its kinship
and continuity with all natural things and especially with the
higher forms of animal life. He seeks basic philosophical cate-

gories that apply alike to men, to animals, to plants and even to stones, molecules and electrons.

Many modern philosophers have believed that if common categories are applied to man and to non-human entities, man must understand himself reductionistically as nothing more than an assemblage of physical parts. To avoid this conclusion a dualism of mind and matter or of spirit and nature has been orthodox in wide circles. Matter or nature is then regarded as the proper object of study in the natural sciences, whose methods are reductionistic and deterministic. But mind or spirit is supposed to be of a fundamentally different order and is treated in terms of its freedom, responsibility, creativity and history.

There has been much justification for this procedure. The natural sciences do tend to seek explanations of the complex patterns of order and movement in nature in terms of the simpler behaviour of the particles of which larger bodies and organisms are composed. Although strict determinism and absolute prediction are no longer the goals of physics, statistical predictions are still sought, and the explanation of psychological phenomena in terms of biology, of biological phenomena in terms of chemistry, and of chemical phenomena in terms of physics still exercises a strong hold on the scientific imagination.

If viewing man as a part of nature necessarily meant sharing in this reductionistic drive, then man would have good reason to maintain his independent self-understanding. But even within the sciences there are strong indications of the inadequacy of this view of their task and of the presence in nature of much that cannot be grasped in their categories. They deal necessarily only with the public world, the world as it can be viewed by a plurality of observers and measured by their instruments. But there is no reason to suppose that nature is only the appearance it presents to man's senses. If, in dealing with our fellow men, we reject the behaviouristic view that they can be reduced to their sensory appearance to us, why should we accept this view when dealing with animals, or for that matter, micro-organisms? If human conscious experience did emerge and now emerges within nature, then nature is far richer than empiricists, idealists, existentialists and phenomenologists have supposed. To seek fundamental categories exemplified both in conscious human experience and in electrons is no more to reduce men to electrons than to raise electrons to the levels of man.

If all we sought were common categories, however, the implications *would* be levelling. Men and electrons would be viewed as being very much alike. And however far we go in attributing reality, value and even inwardness or subjectivity to electrons, we properly resist the idea that these are on the same level as our own.

Whitehead's view of man's place in nature is not levelling in this sense. Kinship and continuity do not imply equality. Man and his conscious experience are *emergents* within nature, and what emerges is something different than, and more than, its sources.

On the other hand, dualists have been wrong in treating this one emergence as the only one. We should not think of all sub-human forms of nature as on an equal plane from which one quite different kind of entity has abruptly emerged. The history of this planet is a history of numerous emergents. One great development was the emergence of the living cell. Another was the emergence of multicellular organisms; another was the emergence of central nervous systems and the accompanying rise of a dominant centre within the organism; another was the emergence of animal consciousness. The emergence of man in his distinctiveness from the other animals may be the greatest of all developments in the history of the earth, but it is continuous with these other emergents and depends upon them.

Along with seeking categories applicable to all things whatsoever, we need to examine the new forms and modes of being that emerge at each level. These two tasks interact. The universal categories must have characteristics that make intelligible the emergence of new forms. The new forms must be displayed as new exemplifications of the universal categories. To see man as an emergent within nature is to see him in his kinship and continuity with all things and in his differences within that continuity. To maintain a proper balance between the vision of man's unity with all things and the insistence upon his peculiarity and uniqueness is a task to which process thought devotes much of its energy. It seeks to do justice to the findings of the natural scientist when he turns his energies to the study of man. It seeks also to do justice to the unique freedom and creativity of man, to man's highest achievements in the realm of the spirit, and to man's strange transcendence over the world. This programme is entailed whenever a philosopher takes *seriously* the view that man is an *emergent within nature*.

Second, in common with process thought generally, Whiteheadians see the emergent as a new kind of process rather than as a substantial thing. The issue here is the nature of the self. Is the self a process, or is it a subject to which, in which, or for which a process occurs? On this point religions and philosophies have divided and continue to divide.

Buddhism split with Hinduism over this question long ago. Hinduism taught a doctrine of Atman as a transphenomenal self. The Atman cannot be identified with the flow of conscious and unconscious experience, or with any part of that flow. What it is can only be approached by the process of negation—not this, not that. Whatever is differentiated is not the Atman. Finally, therefore, the Atman cannot be distinguished from the substantial ground of all things. Atman is Brahman.

Buddhism responded that there is neither Atman nor Brahman. There is no substantial reality underlying the phenomenal flux. There is no self, or subject of experience. There is only the flux or the experience itself.

The same issue can be found in Sartre's debate with Husserl in *The Transcendence of the Ego*. In order to explain how human experience constitutes itself and its world, Husserl found it necessary to posit a transcendental ego. This ego cannot be found within experience. It is inaccessible to phenomenological analysis. But in Husserl's view it is presupposed by that analysis as the ultimate agent which is not itself involved in what it does.

Sartre rejected Husserl's position at this point. There is nothing that constitutes consciousness. There is only the act of constituting. The ego is not the ultimate subject, therefore, but only one of the constituted elements.

Whitehead sides with Buddhism and with Sartre in their joint rejection of an ultimate subject underlying human experience outside the process. But his ontological doctrine allows for more justice to be done to the insistent sense of selfhood than do those of most other process thinkers. Since the human self is not a topic of discussion in Whitehead's own writings, I will postpone major discussion to Section III. However, a brief comment can be made here.

Much more clearly than either Buddhism or Sartre, Whitehead distinguishes what he calls the subjective and the objective poles of experience. When I see a chair or feel an ache in my tooth, I can distinguish between the subjective feeling and that which is felt. Both are within experience, but they are not in experience in the same way. Recognizing that all experience is experience *of* something, Sartre seems to place all the ingredients of this experience on the same plane as constituted objects. Whitehead agrees that all experience is *of* something other than itself. But he shows that, in experiencing the other, we can distinguish *how* it is subjectively felt from its objectivity as other. My feeling of one and the same entity may change in emotional tone—from interest to boredom, for example. Every feeling has both an "objective datum" and a "subjective form". This is true whether the object is an imagined possibility or a definite entity in the actual world. Although there are times when we do think *about* ourselves and thus make ego the object of consciousness—"transcendent" in Sartre's sense—the self is more associated with the continuity of the subjective forms of our feelings than with such objectifications. However, the agreement with Sartre and Buddhism remains. The subjective forms of feelings even in their unity and continuity do not constitute a substantial or transcendental subject of experience. They are fully and wholly within the process of experience.

Third, the kinship and continuity with all of nature implied in this kind of process philosophy goes much deeper than the external one of evolutionary derivation and present dependence. All actuality is experiential in character, and all experience consists in the synthetic inclusion of other experiences. In other words, all actuality is feeling, and all feeling is feeling of other feeling. This flow of feeling constitutes the world.

The main point to be made here is that the feeling that is felt is included in the new feeling. The object passes over into the subject. All real relations are internal. And every experience has real relations with all those other experiences that comprise its given world.

To explain how this can be would require more space than is available here. But the contrast to a substance view should be understandable. If each thing is a substance, then it can have only external relations to all other things. Each substantial thing is what it is in itself and apart from other things. This feature of substance thought passes over into some philosophers who are otherwise process thinkers. It is notable in Sartre, for example, where each "for-itself" seems for ever cut off both from other consciousnesses and from the "in-itself". But in Whitehead's fuller and more consistent process thought, this mutual externality of things is overcome. An experience or event or happening is not self-contained. It comes into being out of its past just by including within itself in a new way the content given it by that past. In the case of a human experience, the dominant past may be past experiences of that same person. These are indeed effectively present in each new moment. But the past that is taken up into the new moment also includes the experience of other human beings and the wider world of nature. Everything that has ever happened makes some contribution, however slight, to all that happens now. We are all quite literally part of each other, and this interconnection and interpenetration unites us not only with our fellow human beings but with the whole natural world.

II

If we are to develop categories that apply to all things, we must overcome the dualism of the mental and the physical. This undertaking is common to all naturalistic process thinkers. Yet Whitehead's way of treating the problem is unique in its richness and adequacy.

Some process thinkers, such as Hume and Dewey, have tended to resolve the mental and the physical alike into a flow of qualities. Others, like Teilhard, have identified it with the distinction of internality and externality, a distinction then attributed to all things. Still others have associated the mental with the centre of dominant control that is present in animals with central nervous systems, and have therefore viewed mentality as an emergent.

Whitehead does justice to all of these approaches but deals

more radically and profoundly with the problem than any. He agrees with Hume and Dewey that we should think of mentality and physicality as qualities within experience or aspects of experience rather than as distinct kinds of entities. He agrees with Teilhard that every entity has both a "within" and a "without", that it is something for itself and something for others. He agrees with Lloyd Morgan and other evolutionists that a distinctive new reality emerged with the central nervous system, and that mentality is peculiarly present in this reality.

But just because all these approaches are correct, none is adequate. The Humean approach cannot do justice to the distinction of internality and externality. To view internality as such as mental is to view it too anthropomorphically; it fails to do justice to the great difference between the internality or subjectivity of the higher animals and that which can be attributed to an electron. But to identify mentality with the higher animals alone is to introduce too radical a break into the evolutionary process; animal mind could not have come into being out of something totally lacking in mind.

Whitehead proposes that we consider every entity, viewed as a process of self-constitution, as having both a physical and a mental aspect. To do so we must think radically about the nature of the mental, and some readers would find it clearer to speak of something proto-mental because they cannot divorce their notion of the mental from features of human experience that Whitehead denies to simpler organisms. For example, for Whitehead mentality does not normally involve consciousness, and thought is still rarer. What he calls mentality is that aspect of all entities whatsoever which in the evolutionary process gradually developed in such a way as to make consciousness and thought possible.

Every entity, as we noted above, takes account of the entities that lie in its past. This universal phenomenon is the ground of all causality. Whitehead speaks of it as "causal efficacy". The flow of the past into the presently self-constituting subject is the physical element in each subject. Thus physicality belongs to the internality of each entity as much as to its externality. The spatio-temporal character of every entity is bound up with its physicality.

But in order to become a new entity out of the welter of material pouring in from the past, each subject must distinguish itself from that past. It must deal with what it receives not merely as the given causal force of the past but as providing the possibilities for its own self-constitution. Hence it must distinguish between the past as it is in itself and the ingredients in the past that constitute possibilities for fresh subjective actualization in the present. In so far as it has to do with possibility as well as with past actuality, every entity has a mental or proto-mental aspect.

In the majority of those entities which we think of as merely physical, this proto-mental aspect leads to nothing more than the repetition of the ingredients given them from the past. But there is no necessity that even very simple entities *merely* repeat the past. The possibilities for self-actualization in each entity need not be limited to the ingredients derived from the past. The fact of emergence in the evolutionary process indicates that novelty is possible. To whatever extent novelty is actualized, life or (we may prefer to say) proto-life appears.

Whitehead explains in detail the degrees and kinds of novelty that are possible. The kinds of novelty that can operate in the subjectivity of an animal are far beyond those that are present in lower organisms. Consciousness depends on these advanced forms of mentality. The complexities of the human organism make possible still different forms of novelty, just those forms, indeed, that constitute the highest reaches of human imagination and speculative thought.

In the ascent of this scale, not only are new and richer forms of novelty actualized, but the relative role of mentality is greatly increased. Electrons are primarily physical entities, and moments of conscious experience are primarily mental. But both an electronic occasion and a human one have both physical and mental elements. Both derive from past actuality, and both constitute themselves as new and distinct entities out of possibility. Both are thus both mental and physical.

The flow of primarily mental experience of which each human being is immediately aware can be called a *psyche*. The psyche can be distinguished from the remainder of the events in the human organism, which are primarily physical and which jointly constitute the body. Hence the distinction of psyche and body within the human organism can and should be made. Much of the traditional mind-body distinction is preserved and reaffirmed in this Whiteheadian analysis, but the term "mind" is misleading and has seriously confused the issues in the past. The use of "mind" falsely implies that the psyche is purely mental and that there is mentality in the bodily events. It also suggests a mental substance that does not exist.

We should understand man, not as the conjunction of a mind with a purely physical body, but as a psychophysical organism. Within this complexly integrated organism there are both psychic and bodily events. The differences between these two types of events are important. A psychic event is not the body-for-itself. It occurs in a definite region of the body—the brain—and is diversely related to events in other parts of the body. This psychic event is not reducible to, or analysable in terms of, bodily events. It is not identical with the brain or with any part of the brain. A psychic event has dimensions radically superior to those enjoyed by any other events in the body. This difference and superiority has understandably given rise to the dualism that has afflicted philosophy and common sense. This dualism is false, but in reaction against it we should not deny the reality and the importance of the distinction.

Whitehead's view of the relation of psychic and bodily events, in harmony with his general ontological position, is interactionist. Psychic events take account of, are causally affected by, incorporate within themselves, and are significantly constituted of bodily events. By virtue of their peculiar capacity to incorporate novelty, they can both be unusually selective in what they take from their bodily environment and remarkably original in the new synthesis by which they constitute themselves. The way they constitute themselves then affects how the bodily environment will act, and through that environment it influences events in the wider world. Since the mutual taking account of each other between bodily and psychic events is simply the exemplification in their case of the universal metaphysical condition of interrelatedness and interdependence, this interactionism introduces none of the philosophical or conceptual problems that have afflicted the interactionist theories of dualists.

Like mentality, *freedom* is also a universal feature of the actual world. Again, what we attribute to simpler entities might better be called proto-freedom since it lacks so many features of human freedom. But freedom is fundamentally self-determination or self-constitution, and it is universally the case that events come into being by an act of self-constitution or decision.

Where possibility is barely distinguishable from the causality of the past, such self-determination has little room for choice. Within very narrow limits, the way in which many entities constitute themselves is predictable in terms of knowledge of their antecedents. As possibility becomes more distinct from causality, that is, as mentality plays a larger role, self-determination becomes more interesting, and the decision for some possibilities against others in the process of self-constitution is more like what we experience as freedom. With the emergence of consciousness and finally of the power of critical reflection the universal act of self-determination becomes human freedom with all its complexity and mystery.

III

Whitehead himself wrote little explicitly and systematically about what theologians call anthropology. What I have said thus far follows sufficiently closely on his work as to be generally acceptable to most students of his thought. However, his philosophy has other implications for a theological understanding of man that are only now being worked out and that are not agreed upon by all interpreters. In this concluding section I shall treat two topics in terms of such implications: (1) man's relation to God, and (2) the question of human nature or the *humanum*.

1. Whitehead was brought to speak of God by his reflection on the relation of events to actuality on the one side and to possibility on the other. An event as a momentary experience cannot determine the relevance to it of the welter of possibilities among which it must choose. In a highly abstract discussion in *Science and the Modern World* Whitehead posited a principle of limitation or concretion enabling entities to achieve the definiteness apart from which there is no actuality. This principle Whitehead called God.

Much of Whitehead's philosophy can be read on the assumption that "God" is a technical term for an abstract speculative concept of little relevance to religious experience or vision. However, Whitehead himself believed otherwise. He called the principle of concretion "God" because he thought that it was in fact the object of religious concern and devotion. He further held that religious experience could be the basis for fleshing out the very limited knowledge of God available to the philosopher. He himself proceeded to carry out this enrichment of the understanding of God in *Religion in the Making*. His further philosophical development led him to a more theistic position.

In *Process and Reality* Whitehead explains that in the origination of every new event or occasion of experience a teleological element is present. Every momentary process of becoming aims at its own completion, and it aims at so completing itself as to attain some value for itself and for its future. It is God who provides the lure of this possible value, as yet unrealized in the actual world. God is thus the source of the "initial aim" of every occasion.

Except in *Religion in the Making* Whitehead's treatment of God as the principle of relevance of possibilities is not particularly related to man or human experience. God is a factor in the occurrence of all processes whatsoever. However, what is true of all processes whatsoever is also true of man, and its meaning for theological anthropology is striking.

Whitehead's doctrine implies that man apart from God is an abstraction. Man cannot be viewed as a self-contained and self-determining being over against God, for in every moment he derives from God an aspect of his being apart from which he cannot exist at all. This means that he is radically dependent on God for his being. But this position should not be confused with another theological anthropology that sees man's being as such as derived from God, while man's mode of actualizing that being is purely autonomous. On the contrary, God bestows being as a directive agency that persuades man towards his good. Since every entity actualizes itself by its own decision in relation to the proffered lure, man is radically self-determined or free, but his freedom is within the context of God's gift. There are rich possibilities here for the understanding of the interrelationship of God's grace and man's freedom.

Whitehead's doctrine strictly implies that every entity what-soever "feels" God. This does not mean that all entities con-sciously experience God. On the contrary, most entities are en-tirely unconscious, and even highly conscious occasions of human experience are largely unconscious. We can at most be aware of a very few of the innumerable entities that impinge upon us and constitute us. Furthermore, consciousness is closely connected with sense experience, and God is never experienced in that way. The doctrine that all entities, including man, always feel God is compatible with the view that there is no conscious experience of God whatever.

However, the denial of the *possibility* of consciousness of God would be quite arbitrary. Whether there are conscious experi-ences of God is, in the context of Whitehead's philosophy, a purely factual or ontic question. If the history of religious experi-ence provides grounds for asserting that such experiences occur, the conditions that are conducive to them are open to investiga-tion. A wide diversity of types of religious experience are subject to explanation in Whitehead's categories. When recognized in their continuity with usually unconscious aspects of experience, they can be removed from a special "supernatural" category, and the prejudice against their authenticity can be reduced. It also becomes possible to judge their relative value both in comparison with ordinary experience and with each other.

Whitehead's insistence that actuality is process rather than substance applies to God as well as to the world. Not only does God penetrate into all that happens in the world but also what happens in the world has its effect upon the divine process as well. Although there are respects in which God is eternal, im-mutable and absolute, in his full concreteness he is a process that is continously open to the world and sympathetically involved with it. In what Whitehead calls God's "consequent nature" God progressively incorporates within himself the values real-ized in the world. What perishes irretrievably in the world is preserved everlastingly in God.

Whitehead was fully aware of the great religious and existen-tial importance of this vision. He saw that the process through which ever new values are realized in the world is at the same time the greatest of evils. It involves perpetual perishing. No sooner does any event occur than it is gone for ever. Every achievement, no matter how great, is past and dead as soon as it is accomplished. Even its effects fade and become insignificant. The full recognition that there are no enduring substances heightens the pathos of this vision of flux. If this were all there is, then the attainment of value is itself of trivial value. Human life would lack significant meaning.

This implies that the sense of the importance of human decisions and the worthwhileness of human action are bound up with belief in God. What we do matters because it makes a difference that is ultimate and everlasting. We live, quite literally, for God.

2. The second topic, with whose consideration this paper will conclude, is the question of human nature or the *humanum*. Much has already been said that bears upon this topic, but its implications have not been fully recognized. In a very important sense there can be for this kind of process philosophy no such thing as human nature.

In part this negation follows from process thought generally. The idea of human nature has associations with the idea of the fixity of species and even of the separate creation of man, which are clearly unacceptable. But if that were the only objection, much of the use of the concept could be salvaged. Even if it were admitted that the constituent elements of human nature came into being gradually and at different points in the evolu - tionary development, still it could be asserted that man as we know him possesses these features in a combination that marks him off sharply from all other forms of life. Religiously, we are interested in man as he now exists. The impossibility of determining at what point in the past we should identify the first humans is irrelevant to our concerns.

A process thinker may well agree with this. There are emergent characteristics of our species that in combination mark us off sharply from all other now existing species. There is no objection in principle to designating these characteristics as human nature.

In practice, however, a problem arises. When great care is exercised to limit the account of human nature to what distinguishes all human beings from all other animals, the results are far less rich than are most descriptions of human nature. These either generalize from a particular culture or assume an essence that functions normatively even when it is factually absent. Usually they do both. I will try briefly to give substance to this charge and to indicate the alternative vision of the human that process philosophy makes possible.

In seeking the distinctiveness of man we can begin with physiology and note such features as the prehensile thumb, the upright posture, the relative lack of hair, the long infancy, the strong and relatively continuous sex drive, and, more important, the capacity of mouth and larynx for highly varied sounds and the relative size of the brain in relation to the body. However, interest in the *humanum* does not focus on the body but on the functions and psychic activities that the body makes possible. When we turn to these, the most striking is the vast range and importance of symbolic activity in man compared with its primitive development in other extant species. Language is the central feature of this human distinctiveness, and most of what is said about human nature depends upon the fact that man speaks.

If all that was meant by human nature was this capacity for language, the minor qualifications required would be quibbles. But it is important to recognize that there is no natural language. This does not mean only that no particular sound is universally associated with particular objects or actions, but much more fundamentally, that the very distinction between objects and actions is not a necessary element in language. Languages express and shape radically different visions of reality, and since the distinctively human is bound up with language, *human* reality, the basic structure of human experience, is thereby rendered diverse.

The fact that man is a speaking animal determines that he will be culturally shaped in a way that no other animal is. Hence we could add cultural conditionedness to our account of human nature. But in view of the usual usage of "human nature" this is paradoxical. We are seeking something that unites all men and offers a norm for determining our common need or destiny. We find that what unites us is the highly abstract fact that unlike animals we are shaped and constituted in fundamentally divergent ways. Whereas much can be said about the behaviour of all members of a particular species of fish, very little can be said about the behaviour of all humans, and most of that turns out to be what we have in common with some other animals. What distinguishes us from other animals turns out immediately to be that we are subject to cultural conditioning in the most diverse ways.

The comparative study of cultures may lead in the end to the discovery of more features that are both common and humanly distinctive than extreme relativists have acknowledged. In that case there can be some enrichment of the concept of human nature. But it is very unlikely that what is common will ever turn out to be what is most important or interesting about man as he is culturally shaped. Hence human nature, empirically understood, can have no significant normative function for philosophy or theology.

This conclusion runs counter to widespread theological practice. Theologians often begin by describing the human situation generally in such a way as to show that Christ or the Christian gospel meets the basic need of man as man. But if there is no common basic need of man as man, then this practice is illusory. It is insufficient, for example, to accept Heidegger's analysis of human existence with its two modes of authenticity and inauthenticity, and then show that Christ and Christ alone makes authenticity possible. Heidegger's analysis turns out to be of one culturally-conditioned type of human existence and inapplicable to others.

Process philosophy, of course, does not encourage us to stop with the identification of a variety of types of human existence. These types may have achieved apparent stability over thousands of years in one culture or another, but such stability is only relative. Structures of human existence arise, develop and are transformed both by internal development and by encounter with others. They have their histories. Traditional structures are today in crisis all over the world. Our task is not to discover what human nature is or has always been. Our task is the formation of new modes of existence. If Christ has universal relevance, it is in terms of a still unrealized future.

Process philosophy provides the assurance that the values of the world are cumulative in God. But it provides no assurance that out of man's present turmoil there will arise a better form of human existence. There is indeed no assurance that the human species will survive in any form. If we do survive it could be under conditions of rigid totalitarian control or of savagery. The immanence of God in the world *is* a ground for hope. But whether we will respond to God's persuasive lure to move forward to the realization of new forms of existence or will lose what we now prize as freedom, imagination and love, depends on human response.

Bas van Iersel

The Normative Anthropology of the Gospel

I. Anthropology and the Gospel

MAN's image changes with that of society. This also applies to the image of man underlying Scripture. There are, of course, several variants of this biblical anthropology, one of which is the lived and experienced anthropology exemplied in different ways in the Psalms and in Ecclesiastes. There are also variants of what may be called a more philosophical anthropology found especially in the New Testament, the two most important forms of which are the monistic anthropology of Semitic thought and the dualistic anthropology of Hellenism. These two ways of thinking are both found above all in the Gospels, in which the words of Jesus reflect the Semitic anthropology, whereas the background to the thinking of the evangelists themselves is frequently Hellenistic.

The importance of this anthropological background to our understanding of Scripture in general cannot be disputed, but what I really want to discuss here is whether it is possible to discern in the Gospels any anthropological values of such lasting importance that they should continue to act as a critical ferment in the Church's witness. In other words, can the anthropology of the Gospel provide us with a normative view of man?

I do not propose to discuss the degree to which the normative anthropology of the Gospel is specifically Christian. To do this, I would have to compare the anthropological data of the Bible with others outside it. This would take me far beyond the scope of this article.

The word "gospel" itself requires a little explanation in this context—the exegete above all is no longer clear what the word really means. The first to use the word in a Christian context was Paul, in whose letters "gospel" means both the proclamation of the Christian message and the content of the message itself. His "gospel" is his proclamation of Jesus Christ, the *kerygma* (Rom. 16. 25–26). Usually linked to brief confessions of faith, this "gospel" is often summarized in a short formula (see Rom. 1. 1–4; 1 Cor. 15. 1–5; 2 Tim. 2. 8) containing the essential datum that Jesus rose again from the dead. At first sight, these formulas apparently contain nothing that could be interpreted as a normative view of man.

The word "gospel", however, also means the "good news" about Jesus and this is what is expressed in the four books we call "the Gospels". These books tell us a great deal about Jesus and they can be regarded as a collection of everything that the authors wanted us to remember in connection with Jesus. They contain short accounts of things that Jesus did and that happened to him as well as various statements he made. These accounts and statements were then set within the structure of a new and longer story, each evangelist making his own selection from the material that was known to him, editing this material at his own discretion and placing it within a chronological and geographical framework. In this way, the four Gospels became four different books.

This difference is particularly striking in the case of the fourth Gospel, but it is also present in all the other accounts, because each author had an obvious preference for certain themes and emphases. For this reason, we cannot simply regard the four Gospels as the one Gospel, although it is in fact possible to distinguish the one Gospel in them, because each aims to keep alive the memory of the one Jesus. This is clear from the fact that the first three are built up on the basis of similar textual material. It is, however, even clearer from the fact that the material that they do not have in common is basically in accordance with one single total picture of what Jesus said and did. We are therefore justified, I believe, not only in asking what normative view of man can be derived from the Gospel, but also in attempting to answer this question, so long as we bear in mind the differences between the various accounts.

I must, however, preface my attempt to do this with two brief comments. Firstly, the reader should not expect any spectacularly new or disturbing pronouncements to be made. If I were to do this it would mean that I had not understood the attempts made during the last twenty centuries to promote the cause of Jesus. Secondly, there has been a great deal of discussion about whether Jesus' statements were addressed to his immediate circle or to all men. As it has so far proved impossible to reconstruct satisfactorily the situation within which Jesus said these words, I shall simply leave out those statements which were quite clearly addressed only to those who were to proclaim the Gospel.

II. The Normative Image of Man and the Image of Jesus

It is clearly not enough to confine one's search for a normative view of man to Jesus' statements about human behaviour. We have also to include the accounts dealing with Jesus himself. Neither can be fully understood without reference to the other; each determines the meaning of the other, and ultimately the image of Jesus was etched into the memory of those who belonged to his community because it expressed for them something, or perhaps even the whole, of a normative image of man.

This connection is also expressed in the epistles. Paul applied the anthropology of the Old Testament first to Jesus and then to man, who, the apostle insisted, reflected the image of God the creator to the extent that he reflected that of Jesus (1 Cor. 15. 49; 2 Cor. 3. 18; 4. 4; Col. 1. 15; 3. 10). Jesus is also shown in other epistles to be the model for man (see especially Heb. 1. 1–4; 1 John 1. 1–3; see also John 1. 9; 10. 30–38; 14. 1–14). In these two passages, Jesus is called the "Son (of God)". This does not mean that he is not presented as a model for man, but that this model has lasting value and cannot be disregarded.

It is clear, then, that christology in the literal sense of the word cannot be ignored in considering the Gospel as a normative anthropology—the anthropology of the Gospel must express what the evangelists say about Jesus. It is also necessary to take into account the problem of the relationship between the historical

Jesus and the kerygmatic Christ. What we are concerned with here is the image of Jesus as preserved in the memory of his community and in the text of the Gospel.

III. THE KINGDOM OF GOD, CONVERSION AND THE SON OF MAN

In considering the human values contained in the Gospel, Jesus' words and actions cannot be divorced from the context, which is defined by the key phrases "kingdom of God", "conversion" and "Son of Man". The *coming of the kingdom of God* is the indicative which underlies all Jesus' words and actions; *conversion* is the imperative underlying all that the Gospel says about man's activity; and *Son of Man* is the name pointing to the man who gave a human aspect to this.

Above all, these three terms establish a link between the present and the future. This is obvious in the case of the coming of the kingdom of God, which is closely connected with human behaviour (see, for example, Luke 7. 22). Man's reaction to this coming is conversion, but Luke has shown that this is not confined to a mere change in attitude in the individual (see Luke 3. 10–14). The name Son of Man was used for Jesus, and the Christian community not only saw Jesus as the coming Son of Man of Daniel 7, but also associated him inseparably with the future kingdom of God. In Matt. 25. 31–46, for example, the future last judgment is closely linked with the actions and omissions of men in the present with regard to the Son of Man.

What is important to notice here, then, is that it would be quite wrong to relate our behaviour as men to the Gospel in the belief that this norm was established in and for the past. On the contrary, everything that the Son of Man said and did as a norm comes to us from the future. Although Jesus' words and actions appear in the Gospels as a divine imperative and there is—in the fourth Gospel especially—constant reference to the significance to Jesus of God's will, this does not mean that his way was clearly marked out for him. On the contrary, the Gospels indicate quite distinctly that, although Jesus spoke and acted in the light of a special vision, all his words and actions corresponded to the demands made by the concrete situation or by people.

Statements by and stories about Jesus have been placed in the

Gospels within the triangle formed by these three key-words. The statements include numerous dynamic rules of human conduct, expressed not as obligatory legal directions, but as appeals. They are obviously dynamic because the normative view of man given in the Gospels is not qualified by nouns or by adjectives describing human qualities, but clearly presupposes a pattern of human relationships. Both the rules of conduct and the accounts of Jesus' words and activities relate to man's—and in the latter case to Jesus'—attitude and behaviour towards his fellow men.

IV. THE GOSPEL ACCORDING TO MARK

The few data providing a normative view of man in Mark are all important. The passage about picking ears of corn on the sabbath, for example (Mark 2. 23–26), is followed by a statement by Jesus, "The sabbath was made for man, not man for the sabbath" (v. 27), which shows us that the real norm for human action is man himself without any further qualification. Any rule of human behaviour is valid only if it promotes man's well-being. This statement by Jesus continues with the words: "The Son of Man is lord even of the sabbath" (v. 28), showing, on the one hand, that the statement about the sabbath being made for man has consequences from which man might recoil, but, on the other, that it points to a relationship between the normative image of man in the Gospel and the image of Jesus that persisted in the primitive Christian community. This is made even clearer by the fact that this passage about man and the sabbath is followed in all three synoptic Gospels by an action by Jesus which underlines this view (Mark 3. 1–5 par.). Jesus' cure of the man with the withered hand is, moreover, given meaning by the words "Is it lawful on the sabbath to do good or to do harm, to save life or to kill?" This second passage describing the cure and its meaning (Mark 3. 1–5) goes even further than the first passage (Mark 2. 23–28), because it shows clearly that to promote the well-being of a fellow man is the highest norm of human behaviour.

In another passage (Mark 7. 1–13), Jesus discusses with the Pharisees the value of the human tradition of declaring something to be an offering ("corban") so that it cannot be used for other purposes, contrasting it with the law of God (vv. 8, 9, 13). What is important, however, is that Jesus' example emphasizes what ought to be done for one's fellow men, in this case for one's father and mother, thus providing a transition from a ritual action of washing hands and various objects to the care of one's fellow men. The second is the valid norm for human behaviour.

The same emphasis is made in all the actions of Jesus recorded in the Gospel; the primitive community clearly remembered Jesus as a man whose activity was entirely oriented towards the people he met on his way. He cured the sick (Mark 1. 23–33, 40–45; 2. 1–12; 5. 21–43; 7. 24–37; 8. 22–26; 10. 46–52), freed men from demonic powers (5. 1–20; 7. 24–30; 9. 14–27), gave food to the hungry (6. 30–44; 8. 1–10), saved men in danger (4. 35–41; 6. 45–51), and ate with sinners (2. 13–17). He was therefore able to say: "Those who are well have no need of a physician" and "I came not to call the righteous, but sinners" (2. 17). He went so far in identifying himself with his unfortunate fellow men that, like a leper, "he could no longer openly enter a town, but was out in the country" (1. 25). The Marcan accounts of Jesus' total dedication to the well-being of others are very different in content from the rabbinical and Hellenistic miracle stories, in which the miracle worker seeks either to justify himself or to stupefy his audience with his magic art. This is something explicitly rejected by Jesus (8. 11–12).

The conversation between Jesus and the rich young man (10. 17–22) and Jesus' subsequent statements about riches (10. 23–31) show that the disciple has to go further than the commandments. The young man who wanted to follow Jesus lacked one thing— he had to sell his possessions and give the money to the poor—and this one thing was and is an essential condition of discipleship.

Even more important in this context are the prophecies of the Passion and the rules of behaviour for the disciples that follow them (Mark 8. 31–38; 9. 30–37; 10. 32–45). The close connection between the gospel image of Jesus as "the Son of Man who came not to be served but to serve, and to give his life as a ransom for many" (10. 45) and the normative image of man, whose rule of life must be "to be last of all and servant of all" (9. 35; see also 10. 43) and to lose his life in total commitment (8. 34–37), is made quite explicit here.

Although the passage about the first commandment in Mark
(12. 28–34) is placed in a less striking context than the three texts
mentioned above and is certainly less far-reaching than the
parallel text in Matthew (22. 34–40), which states that the love
of one's neighbour is equal to the love of God (v. 39) and that
"all the law and the prophets" depend on these two commandments, it is still very important—for two reasons. In the first
place, although the scribe only asks about the first commandment, Jesus' answer includes both the first (the commandment to
love God) and the second (the commandment to love one's neighbour). The meaning is clear—the first cannot be kept without
keeping the second. In the second place, the continuation of the
conversation, which is only found in Mark (12. 32–34), is very
significant. It clearly means that God is not really loved by burnt
offerings and sacrifices, but by loving one's neighbour. This is
precisely the commandment of God, and it is a rule of life which
the scribes and pharisees neglected in the previously mentioned
passage on "corban" (7. 8–9), and which was the one thing lacking in the rich young man of 10. 17–23. We may conclude, then,
that there is only one fundamental rule of human conduct according to Mark—to care for our fellow man who needs us.

There is only one passage in Mark containing a concrete rule
for a specific situation, that of marriage and divorce. In Mark 10.
1–12, we are faced with the question whether indissoluble marriage is an essential human value which cannot be abandoned.
There are, however, powerful reasons for believing that the emphasis is not so much on v. 9 ("What God has joined together,
let not man put asunder") as on v. 11 ("Whoever divorces his
wife and marries another, commits adultery against her", with
the addition referring to the wife divorcing her husband in v. 12),
which is the answer to the question posed in v. 2, the question
that dominates the whole passage: "Is it lawful for a man to
divorce his wife?" Between this question and the answer is an
attempt to justify the real answer in v. 11, which aims to safe-
guard not the indissolubility of marriage, but the well-being of
the wife who loses all her rights if she is repudiated. The most
powerful argument in favour of this interpretation is the peculiar
structure which occurs here and nowhere else in the Old and
New Testaments: "he commits adultery *against* her". What is at

stake here is the right of the wife not to be repudiated by her husband for some arbitrary reason, whether this is done with a certificate of divorce or not. If this interpretation is correct, this passage has a close affinity with others in which Jesus takes the side of people suffering from injustice.

The verses which refer to the indissolubility of marriage as a human value (vv. 6–9) are also closely connected with the rest of the passage. This suggests that the indissolubility of marriage as such is subordinate to the real value emphasized in the passage, that one should be guided by what is good for one's fellow man, in this case, one's partner in marriage. This, then, is a specific concrete example of the more general rules of human behaviour given in the Gospel according to Mark.

V. THE GOSPELS ACCORDING TO MATTHEW AND LUKE

No new elements of the normative anthropology of the Gospel are found in these two Gospels, but there are new emphases and shades of meaning. In the sermon on the plain, for example (Luke 6. 17–49), we find this formula at the very centre of Jesus' discourse: "As you wish that men would do to you, do so to them" (Luke 6. 31). This "golden rule" is very different from similar rules of conduct compiled by the rabbis. The latter were always expressed negatively, whereas the Lucan formula is quite positive.

Matthew makes this positively formulated formula into one of the leading ideas of the whole Sermon on the Mount (see especially Matt. 5. 1–7, 28) and reproduces it as "Whatever you wish that men would do to you, do so to them", adding the short sentence, "this is the law and the prophets" (Matt. 7. 12). He emphasizes the positive aspect by using the words "all that" ("whatever"); at the same time the addition of the short sentence links the golden rule to the previously mentioned fulfilment of the law and the prophets (5. 17–20) by a "righteousness exceeding that of the scribes and pharisees" (5. 20–48). It is certainly not purely by chance that the "most weighty matters of the law" are, in Matthew, "justice and mercy and faith" (Matt. 23. 23). This may be regarded as a thematization of what is expected of other people.

Another factor which must be taken into consideration is this. Although the golden rule does not explicitly say it (we should do to another person not only what he does to us, but what we want him to do), it does suggest that a balance should be kept between what people do to each other. According to the Gospel, nothing less than this is so. The reciprocal relationship between good and evil as a rule of conduct is firmly rejected (Matt. 5. 38–48; Luke 6. 27–35), and it is precisely in this context in Matthew and Luke that the sentence that is absent from Mark occurs: "love your enemies" (Matt. 5. 44; Luke 6. 27, 35). The criterion is not the good or evil that others do to us, but rather what we want those others to do. *Need* in the broadest sense of the word is what is expressed as a criterion for inviting guests to share one's food in Luke 14. 12–14. The guests are not chosen from among those who may give an invitation in return, but from among those who have the greatest need—"the poor, the maimed, the lame and the blind".

Against this background, then, it is hardly surprising that the retention of personal possessions should be condemned in the Gospel and especially by Matthew and Luke. This was quite clear in the passage in Mark discussed above (10. 17–31). The evangelists, moreover, regarded it as wrong to keep not only super-fluous possessions, but the money or property necessary to support life (Matt. 6. 19–34; Luke 6. 25–34). Giving to the poor is no longer simply a question of almsgiving or charity. It is not simply a question of giving away what is no longer needed by the owner, but of giving everything (Matt. 12. 41–44; Luke 21. 1–4). Luke especially emphasizes this (see Luke 5. 11, 28; 14. 33; 18. 22; Acts 2. 44–45; 4. 32–36; the Baptist in Luke 3. 11 speaks only of sharing what one has). Keeping one's possessions is contrary to one of the fundamental rules of life of the Gospel.

Uncertainty whether "one of the least of these my brethren" (Matt. 25. 40, 45) alludes to the Christian who proclaims the message of Christ or to any person in need has led to doubt about applying the description of the King's judgment (Matt. 25. 31–46) as a norm to man's behaviour. I personally believe that there are no really convincing arguments for limiting it to those who proclaim the Christian Gospel. Such reasons cannot be found in Matt. 10. 40–42 either, because this text is conditioned by the word "send", which gives it its special meaning. The word "send" is absent from Matt. 25. 31–46.

If the description of the judgment gives us as a criterion what everyone has done for others in a situation of need, then this is precisely a confirmation of the fundamental value of the normative anthropology of the Gospel that is evident elsewhere—man's behaviour is right or wrong according to the way in which and the extent to which it is oriented towards others and their need.

VI. WHAT ELEMENTS DOES THE GOSPEL PROVIDE FOR A NORMATIVE ANTHROPOLOGY?

The Gospel provides only one fundamental element for a normative view of man, and that is the model of man's absolute involvement with his fellow man in need, the model of complete human solidarity. All the rules of human conduct found in the Gospel can be traced back to this.

Two comments may serve to conclude this article. Firstly, this human solidarity is demanded with greater insistence when the need is greater, and, secondly, it is not based on a utopian situation. On the contrary, it was called for in a society which rejected it in principle. This is quite clear from the concrete circumstances in which Jesus made this solidarity a living reality. It also emerges clearly from the passages in Matthew and Luke in which it was realized in a hostile situation.

Finally, it is worth noting that the primitive confessions of faith contained in the epistles (1 Cor. 15. 3; Rom. 4. 24; 1 Tim. 2. 5; 1 Pet. 2. 21; 3. 18) also reflect this element of a normative anthropology, in stating that Jesus died for us.

Translated by David Smith

Philippe Delhaye

The Contribution of Vatican II to Moral Theology*

I. The End of Post-Tridentine Moral Theology

THE Counter-Reformation saw the establishment of a new type of moral teaching[1] which, having existed for a long time in close conjunction with moral doctrine, eventually supplanted it. It survived into the present century in the form of the traditional manuals. At the beginning of the Council, this view of moral theory had been contested for some thirty years,[2] but the new trends were still unable to win firm recognition. They were even repressed.[3] Three traditionalist authors, Fathers Hürth, s.j., Gillon, o.p., and Lio, o.f.m., were to prepare the pre-conciliar schema *De ordine morali*.[4]

These authors wanted to restore the repressive aspect of the

---

* The following abbreviations are used in this article: AA = *Apostolicam Actuositatem*; AG = *Ad Gentes*; DH = *Dignitatis Humanae*; GE = *Gravissimum Educationis*; GS = *Gaudium et Spes*; IM = *Inter Mirifica*; LG = *Lumen Gentium*; PG = *Perfectae Caritatis*; PO = *Presbyterorum Ordinis*.

[1] P. Delhaye, "Dogme et morale. Un cas de fédéralisme théologique", *Seminarium*, 11 (1971), pp. 295-305; J. Theiner, *Die Entwicklung der Moraltheologie zur eigenständigen Disziplin* (Regensburg, 1970).

[2] Cf. J. M. Casabo-Suque, *La Teologia Moral en San Juan* (Madrid, 1970), pp. 1-17.

[3] J. Leclerq's *L'enseignement de la morale chrétienne* (Paris, 1970) was "withdrawn from sale" by decree of the Holy Office: *Osservatore Romano*, 2 February 1956, pp. 1-2.

[4] Commissio Theologica Concilio Oecumenico Vaticano II apparendo, *Constitutio de ordine morali* (Vatican, 1961). Cf. P. Delhaye, *Dignité du mariage et de la famille, L'Eglise dans le monde de ce temps*, Vol. 2 (*Commentaires, Unam Sanctam*), p. 387.

teaching of Pius XII. Among the errors denounced were subjec-
tivism and situationalism,[5] against which the schema set the
objective and absolute nature of the moral order. This is said to
exist in God and to be communicated to men in two ways. The
first is that of the commandments of the natural law as confirmed by Christ.[6] The second is the evangelical law, whose tenor
depends on the three counsels.[7] This moral theology would seem
to have two levels (as the Reformed churches objected in regard
to the post-Tridentine Roman Church). It is hardly surprising
that there is no mention of charity, since casuistic moral theology
had constantly opposed it.[8] But the *De ordine morali* went even
further, and actually expressed a fear that a moral theology of
charity would mean no more than verbalism, sentimentalism
and an abandonment of moral precepts.[9] There was a decidedly
firm attempt to refute the idea that charity is the only valid basis
of Christian morality and the necessary condition for merit.[10]

[5] The text did not make the necessary distinctions, cf. E. Schillebeeckx,
Approches théologiques, Vol. 2 (Paris, 1965), p. 247, for the debate on
situation ethics.

[6] *De Ordini Morali*, 4: ". . . Loquens autem per Filium suum, qui
praecepta Decalogi, gentibus quoque naturaliter licet imperfectius inno-
tescentia, non venit solvere sed adimplere, legem naturalem restauravit,
dilucidavit, perfecit, sanctificavit et ad altiorem ordinem evexit."

[7] *De Ordine Morali*, 5: "Continet autem ordo moralis propter gratiam
Christi apparet in lege evangelica: praescripta, vetita, permissa, consilia.
Insigne eius gloriosum notaque distinctiva est via perfectionis illa chris-
tiana, qua fideles a Deo vocati in consiliorum evangelicorum observatione
Christum pauperem, castum, ad mortem usque oboedientem, quam
proxime sequi eique quam maxime adsimilari conantur."

[8] Two factors have played a part in this historical evolution. Minimalism
forced the casuists to reduce the number of "acts" of charity (Denzinger,
2021, 2105–2107, 2290). They took advantage of the condemnations of
Fénelon (pure love) and the Jansenists (need for an explicit intention of
charity in each action) to adopt extreme positions.

[9] *De Ordine Morali*, 15: "Nec minus cavendum est, ne simplices, adagio
illo: 'Ama et fac quod vis' male intellecto, falso credant nonnisi unum
praeceptum, videlicet: *Diliges* in christiana vita esse retinendum. Talis
enim vita ad incertum quendam amoris affectum reduceretur, neglecta
omnino praeceptorum observantia, contradicente ipso Domino: 'Si vis ad
vita ingredi, serva mandata' " (Matt. 19. 17).

[10] In this text, Fr Hürth is above all confident of being able to defend
the curious opinion of Vasquez according to which no charitable motive
(even one that is wholly virtual or habitual) is necessary for the Christian
moral life. Cf. J. Abel, *L'influence de la charité sur les actes moraux dans
une controverse posttridentine* (Louvain Univ. thesis, 1970).

The conciliar majority obtained in November 1962 rejected this text. It was dropped with the rest of the preparatory commissions' schemata. There are several reasons why it was not replaced with a new text. The history of the Council shows that the major texts adopted by Vatican II derive from the preceding theological efforts. This is the case for liturgy, ecclesiology and exegesis. But the movement towards the renewal of moral theology as good as disappeared.

In fact there were hardly any moral theologians at the Council. Those bishops who specialized in theology had taught mainly exegesis and dogma. The selection of the *periti* almost entirely eliminated the very small number of moral theologians who favoured the new tendencies apparent in the preparatory Commissions. Time was needed to choose some new ones. Almost immediately, they were set to work on *Gaudium et Spes*.

The consequences of the foregoing were, paradoxically, fortunate. The former casuistic moral theology disappeared almost completely. A new expression of the moral imperatives of the faith was to be found which enjoyed continuity with Scripture, dogma and the life of the Church: in short, by re-establishing contacts which the advocates of a renewed moral theology had hardly dared to suppose could be restored.

II. Life in Christ

The moral theology of the texts centred upon a legalistic obligation based on a canonist casuistics and, sometimes, natural law. There was only one apologetical target: an answer to the philosophy of the (German) Enlightenment. There was also a recognition of those sacralizing tendencies of the Middle Ages which identified natural law with the Gospel.[11] Vatican II hardly had recourse to this idea.[12] On the contrary, it saw the source of the

---

[11] Cf. P. Delhaye, *Permanence du droit naturel*, second edition (Louvain, 1967), pp. 68 ff. The first lines of the *Decretum Gratiani* virtually identify natural law with the Mosaic and evangelical laws.

[12] Mgr Delacroix's very full summary notes only six references to natural law. On the other hand, the Council splits this hybrid concept up into several elements: the first principles of conscience as inscribed in the heart of man (Rom. 2. 14) (GS 16, 23); moral philosophy; international law established by reason and conscience (*ius naturale gentium*) (GS 79); moral

renewal of Christian moral thought as lying in the Bible.[13]

Henceforth the moral life appeared under two aspects: the ontological and the psychological. The Christian life was essentially a gift from Christ and the fruit of the Spirit (LG 7).[14] Moral demands became more the normal development of a new state than obedience to an external imperative. Yet the Gospel and divine law do reveal to us what we are and what we ought to become: "The heritage of this (Christian) people is the dignity and freedom of the sons of God, in whose hearts the Holy Spirit dwells as in his Temple. Its law is the new commandment to love as Christ loved us (cf. Jn. 13. 34)" (LG 9). "Therefore Christ the Lord . . . commissioned the apostles to preach to all men that gospel which is the source of all saving truth and moral teaching . . ." (DV 7). God calls man to place himself in the history of salvation and in human history in terms of values set forth in his covenant. Vatican II does not forgo the use of the word "law", but in the very wide sense in which Paul speaks of the law or "principle of faith" (Rom. 3. 27) and of the law of Christ (Gal. 6. 2). Hence the conception of the law as a framework replaces the idea of the precise law (see, e.g., LG 9; GS 22, 24, 28, 32, 38, 41, 42, 43, 48, 50, 51, 78, 89).

Any extrinsicism is all the more excluded inasmuch as the law is taken up by Christian consciences enlightened by the Spirit (LG 12). The conscience, the innermost standard of behaviour (GS 16, 19, DH 3), should search out the truth according to its own dynamism (DH 3). It runs the risk of being clouded by sin (GS 16) and should be actively cultivated (DH 3). The

---

laws arising from the nature of things (AA 17, IM 11); the use of reason and recourse to culture in studying the moral theology of the Gospel (GS 57, 59, GE 8).

[13] This is also the essential directive in this regard according to *Optatam totius* 16: "Specialis cura impendatur theologiae morali perficiendae, cuius scientifica expositio, doctrina S. Scripturae magis nutrita, celsitudinem vocationis fidelium in Christo illustret eorumque obligationem in caritate pro mundi vita fructum ferendi." Cf. B. Häring, *La morale après la concile* (Paris, 1967); J. Fuchs, *Le renouvau de la théologie morale selon Vatican II* (Tournai, 1968).

[14] P. Delhaye, "L'Esprit saint et la vie morale du chrétien d'après *Lumen Gentium*", *Ecclesia a Spiritu Sancto edocta: Hommage à Mgr G. Philips* (Gembloux, 1970), pp. 432–43.

teaching Church will lay down the detailed practicalities of faith (LG 25).

In this regard the Council inaugurated a new style in the exercise of the magisterium. It did not formulate any definitions or condemnations but gave priority to those truths of faith which are essentially relevant to life. The pastoral teaching of the Church (GS note 1) includes both doctrinal principles and the transitory events which are to be viewed in their light. Its disciplinary operation puts more trust in the presentation of essential values than in the multiplication of detailed instructions (PC 4). Hence it requires laymen to look to their own responsibilities in various areas (GS 43, esp. 50).[15]

III. A MORAL THEOLOGY OF CHARITY

A moral theology which is located at the level of grace, inwardness and values can only increase the role of faith, hope and charity, *tria haec* (1 Cor. 13. 13). In this way, spontaneously and coherently, the forecast of some advocates of a renewed moral theology was realized; the Christian ethos is to be formulated according to the requirements of theological virtues:[16] "Seeking after the glory of Christ, the Church becomes more like her exalted model, and continually progresses in faith, hope and charity, searching out and doing the will of God in all things" (LG 65). Charity is present throughout the *corpus Vaticanum*, but reasons of space will allow concentration only on Chapter V of *Lumen Gentium*. It gives a direct answer to *De ordine morali* in refusing a "two-level morality" and in recalling that the demands of Christianity are summed up for us all in charity. The evangelical counsels are only a privileged way of attaining to that end (LG 45). This teaching is also a protest against the Pelagian tendencies of casuistics,[17] inasmuch as it locates Agape

[15] I have tried to characterize in detail this new style of the magisterium in an article which will appear shortly.

[16] Despite necessary recourse to a thirteenth-century expression, I prefer the viewpoint of the twelfth century, which—here above all—points to dynamic graces. Cf. P. Delhaye, *Rencontre de Dieu et de l'homme*, Vol. 1 (Paris, 1956), p. 119.

[17] P. Delhaye, "Le kerygme de la charité à Vatican II", *Revue théologique de Louvain*, 1 (1970), pp. 144-74.

primarily in God and shows that we participate in it through grace (Rom. 5. 5, recalled in LG 42). "Thus the first and most necessary gift is that charity by which we love God above all things and our neighbour because of God" (LG 42). It is necessary "by God's gifts" to "hold on to and complete in [our] lives this holiness which [we] have received...to possess the fruits of the Spirit unto holiness" (LG 40). "If that love, as good seed, is to grow and bring forth fruit in the soul, each one of the faithful must willingly hear the word of God and with the help of his grace act to fulfil his will. Each must share frequently in the sacraments, the Eucharist especially, and in liturgical rites. Each must apply himself constantly to prayer, self-denial, active brotherly service, and the exercise of all the virtues" (LG 42).

IV. MORAL THEOLOGY OF FAITH

The promotion of charity implies that of faith, for, according to Paul (Gal. 5. 6), they act in concert. Faith arises from Christ's call: it is the word of salvation which awakens faith in non-Christians' hearts and which nourishes it in the hearts of Christians: "So faith comes from what is heard, and what is heard comes by the preaching of Christ" (Rom. 10. 17; PO 4). This preaching was entrusted to the apostles, to their successors and to their co-workers, in order to save men by uniting them in the Church (LG 14; AG 7, 21).

Man's response is personal, free and committed. In proclaiming religious liberty, Vatican II reaffirms that "...man's response to God in faith must be free.... Man, redeemed by Christ the Saviour and through Christ Jesus called to be God's adopted son, cannot give his adherence to God revealing himself unless the Father draw him to offer to God the reasonable and free submission of faith" (DH 10).

In "looking with faith to Jesus the author of salvation" (LG 9, AG 13), man makes a first moral commitment:[18] The obedience of faith is due to God who reveals (Rom. 16. 16; Rom. 1. 5; 2 Cor. 10. 5-6); the obedience to which man surrenders himself wholly and freely to God—"entirely submitting intellect and will

---

[18] J. Mehl, *Ethique protestante et éthique catholique* (Neuchâtel, 1970).

to God who reveals" (Vatican I) and voluntarily assenting to the revelation that God makes (AG 5). It should be noted that the twenty-first Council lays much more emphasis than did the intellectualist theology of the nineteenth century on "the interior help of the Holy Spirit"..."moving the heart and turning it to God" (*Dei Verbum* 5).

All faith is conversion, more especially so at the first moment of adherence to Christ but also in its permanent effect (AG 13). To believe is to adhere to the one who is the way, the truth and the life (Jn. 14. 6); it is to turn away from sin in order to enter into the mystery of love of God which calls man to enter into personal relations with him in Christ. Faith is the source of action since it introduces man to the paschal mystery, and makes him abandon the old for the new man who finds his perfection in Christ. A change of mind takes place gradually. Faith leads to baptism as to all the sacraments, for which Vatican II uses the patristic formula "the sacraments of faith" (LG 21).

One can see how the expression "morality of faith"[19] is to be taken. Faith not only gives a new view of things which implies a new form of behaviour, but is a perpetual suasion to conversion. This dynamism of faith is constantly referred to by Vatican II (LG 12) when speaking of the *sensus fidelium* which, it says, enables the people of God to penetrate "more deeply by accurate insights" the "faith once delivered to the saints", and to apply "it more thoroughly to life". The action of the Spirit is mediated through faith in order to enliven even the earthly life of Christians: "...the promised restoration which we are awaiting has already begun in Christ, is carried forward in the mission of the Holy Spirit, and through him continues in the Church. There we learn through faith the meaning, too, of our temporal life, as we perform, with hope of good things to come, the task committed to us in this world by the Father, and work out our salvation" (LG 48).

The formula of GS 15 covers all (individual, social and political) morality: "It is...through the gift of the Holy Spirit that man comes by faith to the contemplation and appreciation of

---

[19] P. Delhaye, "L'emprise de la foi sur la vie normale", *Supplément de la vie spirituelle*", 55 (1960), pp. 375-414.

the divine plan." Other passages in GS comment on this: "... faith throws a new light on everything, manifests God's design for man's total vocation, and thus directs the mind to solutions which are fully human" (GS 11). The connections between faith and culture are given special attention (GS II, 2). The following formulation, from GS 58, shows how revelation accepted by faith modifies the whole of man's life, even in matters secular: "The good news of Christ constantly renews the life culture of fallen man. It combats and renews the errors and evils resulting from sinful allurements which are a perpetual threat. It never ceases to purify and elevate the morality of peoples. By riches coming from above, it makes fruitful, as it were from within, the spiritual qualities and gifts of every people and of every age. It strengthens, perfects and restores them in Christ. Thus by the very fulfilment of her own mission the Church stimulates and advances human and civil culture. By her action, even in its liturgical form, she leads men towards interior liberty." GS 2 outlines the programme for a conscientious and radiant life of faith. In the faith, young people come to learn the meaning of praise of God, and are trained to conduct their personal lives "in righteousness and in the sanctity of truth, according to [their] new standard of manhood" (Eph. 4. 22–24). In this way they bear witness to the hope that is in them and participate in the Christian transformation of the world thanks to which "natural values, viewed in the full perspective of humanity as redeemed by Christ, may contribute to the good of society as a whole".

Vatican II yielded to the constant and usual temptation of all moralists in treating hope as a poor relation. There is not much explicit teaching on this point. Nevertheless, it is one of the vital aspects of the ethos of the twenty-first Council, one which enabled it to make Christians more attentive to the eschatological nature of the kingdom of God (LG 48) and to insist on commitment to this world (GS 43).

V. Openness to Earthly Reality and Human Values

Three important teachings in this regard partly concern the moral theologian. (1) All moral ultimates were formerly referred to everlasting happiness. Descended from the polemics of another age, *De fine ultimo* harshly criticized all human values which were supposed rivals. Life in this world appeared only as a testing period (*in hac lacrimarum valle*). A more or less emphatic *contemptus mundi* was the orientation of Christian asceticism and moral theology. Only twenty years before the Council did a movement in favour of a theology of earthly reality make itself apparent.

Vatican II justified this trend and, grounding itself in the experience of the Christian life, affirmed that the search for human values (AA 7) in regard to the ultimate goal does not take place on the level of means (AA 7). It is necessary to make a distinction in moral theology between a primary end (divinization) and a secondary end (humanization) (GS 40, 42, 43, 57). Six reasons are given for this secular commitment: the fundamental goodness of creation, the dignity of man, the diaconate of charity, "recapitulation" in Christ, his example, and the cosmic relevance of the Resurrection (AA 7, GS 43, 45, 58).[20]

(2) A Christian anthropology is outlined in the first three chapters of GS, in answer to the often expressed requests for a *De homine*. The three stages in which it is developed contain several moral elements. In regard to the person, there is a recurrence of the theme of the image of God (GS 12) which was so often the basis of patristic moral theology. Man who is free (GS 17) can destroy this resemblance by sinning (GS 13), by not following the verdict of his conscience, and by rejecting God instead of accepting the Creator's and Redeemer's call (GS 22).[21] Secondly, the common good no longer seems oppressive. It consists of the "sum of those conditions of social life which allow social groups and their individual members relatively thorough and easy access to their own fulfilment" (GS 26). An individualistic ethics is out of date (GS 30). Christ is the summit of human solidarity (GS 32), who is realized in a charity (GS 24) extended even to one's enemies (GS 28). Respect for human rights (GS 26, 27), an understanding of interdependence (GS 25), social

[20] P. Delhaye, *Le dialogue de l'Eglise et du monde* (Gembloux, 1968), pp. 113-42; "Bonheur et morale", *Catéchistes*, 68 (1966), pp. 333-52.
[21] P. Delhaye, "La dignité de la personne humaine", in G. Barauna, *L'Eglise dans le monde de ce temps* (Paris, 1968), pp. 344-68.

justice (GS 29), and co-responsibility and participation (GS 31) are the "major truths" listed by *Gaudium et Spes* as those from which all may draw the necessary consequences (GS 23). A third dimension of human anthropology is located in reflection on commitment in the secular world. Recognition has to be given to an autonomy proper to earthly reality (GS 36), but, on the other hand, faith and grace purify human activity (GS 37). Christ is the ultimate towards which the history of salvation and human history both tend (GS 39).

(3) The second part of *Gaudium et Spes* is little short of a "treatise on values"; it covers family, cultural, economic, social, political and international life. The former *De matrimonio* and *De iustitia* are replaced with profit. Instead of attempting a detailed analysis (which the various commentaries on *Gaudium et Spes* provide anyway), I shall merely note the change in perspective. The obsessive detection and assessment of sins have disappeared. Moral values are no longer things only to be presented; they now exist in continuity with intellectual, emotional and social, i.e., human and cultural, values. The viewpoint is no longer individualistic but communitarian. There is a recognition of the fact that structural reforms are needed to apply moral imperatives. A new collaboration between theology and the human sciences is sketched out. The aim is no longer to constitute a homogeneous area in the sense of "natural law", but to distinguish two different contributions. Family life, culture and political life are autonomous human realities which have their own proper consistencies. The role of Christian moral theology is to bring to bear on the very inwardness of these facts the viewpoint of faith, the dynamism of charity and the power of Christian grace, the better to elicit the deep meaning of these very facts and allow them even greater realization.

Translated by John Griffiths

Walter Hollenweger

The Quest for Authenticity
in Solidarity Groups

LAYTON P. ZIMMER tells of a conversation he had immediately after his ordination with some parish priests. "They asked me to tell them honestly what I thought of 'Sunday morning'. I mustered up my honesty and admitted that I was still dismayed by the fact that, for all their moments of ceremonial glory, Sunday mornings were personal hell because of all the façades that had to be assumed in order to be at least something pleasant to everybody—including those who talked about 'niggers', sterilizing the poor, and preventive H-bombing of Russia. There was a pause in the conversation, and I was afraid that I had offended my seniors. Then one older priest smiled in a kind of sad way and I, covering, asked too loudly what *they* thought of 'Sunday mornings'. More silence! Then a cough, and one said, 'The Church, to me, is small groups of intimate friends getting together, having supper, and just being there a while with each other. At least this is real and it helps us all. Sunday mornings don't, very often, help anybody, do they?'"[1]

That is an analysis which is familiar to many priests, inside and outside parishes. The underground churches, the solidarity groups—or, as they have been calling themselves more recently in the United States, the "free churches" (not to be confused with the "Free Churches")—are trying to describe *theologically*—"as Church"—what has for them in experience the quality of Church. The key word is "community", but community *for a purpose*,

[1] L. P. Zimmer, "The People of the Underground Church", in M. Boyd, *The Underground Church* (New York, 1968; London, 1969), p. 24.

68

not for the sake of community: "a small intense community gets people so close together that the destructive forces in them are free to interact, and then blows itself apart like a nuclear device by implosion. Community for the sake of community is disastrous. It must exist for the sake of some job to be done, which acts as energy field to neutralize the forces of repulsion."[2]

This community also includes people outside the institutional Church, "but always under the authority of Jesus".[3] They are groups in which the demons of violence and exploitation are driven out: "If we see demons being cast out, it doesn't matter whose name it's done in. . . . When we see the dark powers being overcome, we know that nothing but the finger of God can be at work. In that case once again—and now in a radically new historic conjunction—we have to say that the Kingdom of God has come upon us."[4] Such a testimony means (in the U.S.A., Russia and elsewhere) *martyria* in both senses of the word. In fact many Christians from the underground churches have been imprisoned or killed. Others were threatened with torture or the removal of their children.[5] But they prefer to be fools in the world's eyes rather than successes.

I. The Underground Church in the U.S.A.

The best introduction to the underground church in the U.S.A. is provided by its liturgy, significantly called the "covenant of peace" (Ezek. 34. 25). What liturgists have been asking for for a long time, a liturgy "which makes the faithful listen to the service because it expresses their current preoccupations",[6] is methodically carried out in this liturgy, with prayers, formularies and readings which originate in constant exchange with the missionary people of God, and will therefore also be subjected to constant change in the future—which does not imply an abandonment of biblical and ecclesial tradition. The baptismal liturgy,

---

[2] J. P. Brown, *The Liberated Zone. A Guide to Christian Resistance* (Richmond, Va., 1969), p. 161.
[3] J. P. Brown, *op. cit.*, p. 196.
[4] *Ibid.*
[5] L. P. Zimmer, *op. cit.*, p. 26.
[6] Th. Klauser, *Kleine abendländische Liturgiegeschichte* (Bonn, 1965), p. 59.

for example, is called "receiving a baby into the covenant" or (when an adult is being baptized) "going through the waters". This baptism symbolizes "washing off the number of the beast",[7] and this may (not "must") afterwards be practically expressed by burning one's draft card. The Good Friday liturgy is called "a lament for victims and executioners", the liturgy of Christmas "the sanctuary of peace", the eucharistic celebration "the freedom meal". The invocation of the saints begins with the "bridegroom of poverty, our brother Francis, follower of Jesus and friend of the creation". It includes, among others, Gandhi, "apostle of non-violence, reproach to the churches", "Good Pope John, friend of the poor, who longed for the unity of all people", the "peacemakers", Dag Hammerskjøld and Albert Luthuli, Buddha Gautama, "mask of Christ" and "fountain of compassion", John of Patmos, "visionary and apostle, resister to the World Beast", Dante, Bunyan and Isaac Watts, "visionaries and poets, pilgrims of the inner light", Mary Magdalene, "faithful harlot, first witness of new life", Bach, Mozart and Beethoven, "who speak the soul's language", Darwin and Teilhard de Chardin, "students of the earth, voyagers in the past and in the future", Einstein, Marx and Freud, "children of the synagogue", Menno Simons and George Fox, "explorers in the Gospel, generals in the warfare of the Lamb", the confessors of Africa (Augustine), Russia (Pasternak), American (King), Germany (Bonhoeffer) and the "confessors in flames" (Alice Hertz, Jan Palach, Thich Quang Duc), the innocents of Coventry, Dresden and Hiroshima, Socrates, the hippy from Athens, the "unwed mother, blessed Mary wellspring of our liberation". The litany culminates in praise of "our hero and leader, Jesus the manual labourer, root of our dignity, the prophet, who resisted the Establishment, the Liberator, a king because first a servant, the poet, who laid down a new form of speech, Jesus, the Son of God, bright cornerstone of our unity in a new Spirit".[8] The authors write: "We have tried to avoid celebrating the wrong things, like Cranmer, or (worse) cele-

[7] J. P. Brown, op. cit., p. 191.
[8] J. P. Brown and R. L. York (Eds.), The Covenant of Peace. A Liberation Prayer Book by the Free Church of Berkeley (New York, 1971), pp. 33–5; cf. also Win With Love! A Directory of the Liberated Church in America (currently obtainable from Free Church Publications, Box 9177, Berkeley, Calif. 94709).

brating nothing at all, like group sensitivity liturgies on the one hand and the COCU liturgy on the other."[9]

The "free churches" say of themselves: "We are unwilling to say that we are the Church as distinguished from the struggle; we are unwilling to say that we are another political group. One purpose of this book is to challenge the legitimacy of that question. The Church in our groups exists without a central administration, without a budget, without lists of members. It is a movement in the churches and exists in every place where the Holy Spirit works."[10]

II. THEOLOGY IN A MINOR KEY

The political topics which come up in the liturgy are occasions "for a mixture of celebration and penitence".[11] There is no trace of a naïvely optimistic world view—this is no re-issue of a liberal social gospel! It is—as its authors themselves put it—"theology in a minor key",[12] but none the less a minor *melody*. It is a thoroughly eschatological liturgy which, *in the face of the realities*, refuses to make these (ecclesiastical and political) realities the basis of its faith. The basis of its hymn of hope is "Jesus, the manual labourer", who inspires a faith for which more things are possible than what we see. This does not mean that they overestimate their own potential; they admit that "the real agents of reconciliation may come from some unexpected source, a small neutralist power; we'll do well to recognize them when they show up".[13]

It is a church for those who have realized that we are strangers here, that our city is elsewhere. Here we live "in occupied territory" and therefore look round for a "resistance group".[14] Sin is precisely described, for example as the lack of modesty of those economists who "haven't yet learned from the ecologists that a constantly expanding economy is unsuitable for a sphere of finite

[9] J. P. Brown and R. L. York, *The Covenant of Peace*, p. 8.
[10] *The Covenant of Peace*, p. 5.
[11] *The Covenant of Peace*, p. 9.
[12] J. P. Brown, *The Liberated Zone*, p. 7.
[13] *The Liberated Zone*, p. 118.
[14] *The Liberated Zone*, p. 13.

area".[15] Or "what we call the Free World is the area of American business enterprise".[16]

There is a dual attitude towards the established church. The New Testament *ekklesia* is defined as the area in which no compromises are necessary. In the State, on the other hand, compromises are necessary. But "one State is enough. The saints didn't go to all that trouble just to make a little tyranny inside the big one".[17] But the established church cannot be abandoned by the solidarity groups. That would contradict their policy of peace and reconciliation.[18] That is why even a bishop can recognize the necessity and value of the underground church.[19]

Since the United States and Russia are growing together in their efforts at domination and their military policy, the underground church feels that similar peace movements are necessary in Russia.[20] Do such movements exist? They do, even if in a different form from those in the United States.

III. THE UNDERGROUND CHURCH IN THE U.S.S.R.

It is well known that from Tolstoy and Dostoievsky to Pasternak and Solzhenitsyn, the ideas of "peacemakers" and of "an area in which no compromise is necessary" have been alive in Russia. In the United States the churches claimed for themselves a monopoly of representing this message of peace, while in Russia the Communist Party plays this role. In both cases the ideologies of the party (the Church) have been linked with the power apparatus of the State. But in both cases protest groups came into being which rejected this "little tyranny inside the big one". The handwritten and typewritten literature (*samizdat*) on these subjects, which has circulated in Russia for some time, is also known in the West. The solidarity groups in Russia, like those in the U.S.A., include groups of Christians (Orthodox[21] and Pro-

---

[15] *The Liberated Zone*, pp. 20, 29.
[16] *The Liberated Zone*, p. 30.
[17] *The Liberated Zone*, p. 163.
[18] *The Liberated Zone*, p. 183.
[19] P. Moore, "A Bishop Views the Underground Church", in *The Underground Church*, pp. 221-37.
[20] *The Liberated Zone*, pp. 41, 106.
[21] Cf. for instance the very fine letter of A. E. Levitin-Krasnov to Pope Paul VI: in Russian in *Religija i ateizm v SSSR* (March 1970), pp. 1-17;

testants) as well as people who confess no allegiance to any church but are still confessors and martyrs of this covenant of peace and often explicitly invoke the Gospel.

1. *Initiativniki*

Among these solidarity groups there should also be included the so-called initiative group or *initiativniki*, a protest group, partly inside and partly outside the officially recognized All Union of Gospel Christians/Baptists/Pentecostalists. A large proportion of the *initiativniki* are Pentecostalists.[22] They speak with tongues and pray with the sick, and have tried to hold spontaneous meetings—what in America would be called demonstrations—in public places (once even in front of the Kremlin) and in the public transport system. They have come into conflict not only with the Russian State, but also with the ecclesiastical establishment. For the ageing leaders of the Baptist Union the present situation compared with the past is an advance which they are unwilling to jeopardize lightly. The young enthusiasts, however, make comparisons, not with the past, but with what the Fathers of Communism promised. In Western writing on the subject there has been much discussion about whether agents of the State Council for Religious Affairs (CARC), or even of the secret police are active. The former is possible in view of an interview given by Mikhail Zhidkov—the second most important man in the organization.[23] But even without direct state intervention in the ecclesiastical establishment, the Russian *initiativniki* have to pay for their testimony, yet repression cannot quench their testimony.

For example, between 24 and 27 December 1963 four Christians were tried. They were convicted of having admitted minors to their solidarity group and having persuaded believers to neglect their civic duties, not to obey police auxiliaries, not to join a trade union, to hold illegal prayer meetings at night in unhealthy

---

English version in *Religion in Communist Dominated Areas* 9/19–20 (October 1970), pp. 151–8.

[22] Evidence in W. J. Hollenweger, *The Pentecostals* (London and Minneapolis, 1971).

[23] St Durasof, *The Russian Protestants. Evangelicals in the Soviet Union: 1944–1964* (Farleigh Dickinson University Press), p. 202.

conditions and with minors present. When the Baptist Central Committee intervened, the elder members of the community had given way, but the younger ones continued to hold secret meetings. They were sentenced to between three and five years' imprisonment.[24]

One of those convicted, Nikolai Kuzmich Khmara, died of the effects of torture after two weeks in prison: "The palms of his hands were burned; as were his toes and the soles of his feet. The lower part of his abdomen showed marks of deep wounds made by the insertion of a sharp, jagged object; his right leg was swollen; the ankles of both legs seemed to have been beaten; on his body were black and blue bruises."[25]

The 120 members of the community who signed the description of Khmara's dead body quoted above expressed their grief at the horrible death of their brother, who had been converted only in the summer of 1963 from a life "of uninterrupted drunkenness". But they were also strong enough to sing at Khmara's grave and to bear witness: "Do not fear those who only kill the body, but cannot kill the soul." The document signed by the 120 members of the community also includes an important detail from the indictment. One of the charges against the *initiativniki* was that they had "analysed various biblical texts, permitted arbitrary and incorrect interpretations, criticized and did not accept the new constitution of the AUCECB (the Baptist Central Committee)".[26]

"One might think that the witnesses were members of the Holy Synod, people with higher theological education, well versed in biblical truths and called to defend their purity. But not at all! ... Since in the Penal Code there is no article against incorrect interpretation of the Bible, the prosecutor called it reactionary activity, harmful to society. Thus he put 'incorrect' interpretation of the Bible and criticism of the constitution of the AUCECB under Article 227 of the Penal Code."[27]

[24] *Sovetskaya Yustitsia* 9 (1964), p. 27; English in M. Bourdeaux, *Religious Ferment in Russia. Protestant Opposition to Soviet Religious Policy* (London and New York, 1968), pp. 77-8.
[25] Duplicated letter of 120 brothers and sisters from Barnaul and Kulunda (Siberia), 16 February 1964; English: *Religion in Communist Dominated Areas* 3/16 (30 September 1964), pp. 122-5.
[26] *Ibid*.   [27] *Ibid*.

2. The Question of Man

Although the text quoted says nothing direct about the form of biblical interpretation practised by the *initiativniki*, it is nevertheless clear that they risk their lives in order to work out their own interpretation of the Bible. Perhaps oral tradition is more important for an understanding of the theological dimension of these solidarity groups—as with the Independent Zionists of South Africa and the Pentecostalists of Latin America. This oral tradition does leave literary traces, in hymns. Some of these are in our possession. As an example I quote a hymn which begins with modern man at the mercy of technology:

> *Man*
>
> Man, whose life is a perpetual struggle,
> For whom life means a conquest,
> You have subdued all in this world
> But you have failed to subdue yourself.
>
> You have gained fame as a ruler on land,
> You have penetrated the depths of the sea,
> You have reached the heights, but you are still a slave
> To your own base passions.
>
> You have split the invisible atom,
> You know even how to conquer space,
> You have reached the age of great discoveries,
> But you have failed to conquer yourself.
>
> Yes, you are strong and at the same time weak,
> You are great, as well as insignificant,
> By the power of your mind you are a god,
> But by your lust you are a slave.
> You were high, but how low you have fallen.
>
> . . . .
>
> Without your space-ships and all your efforts,
> The Lord will transform your body.
> In the first resurrection he will
> Give an immortal body to the faithful saints.

God is spirit, and the eternal ruler of the stars,
And if you want to reach the starry sky
You must fall down before him, earthbound man,
And you must conquer yourself in this life.[28]

One pictures a young member of the Komsomol who goes over to the *initiativniki* because he is getting bored in the Komsomol.[29] This is not just an inference from the new songs, which, just like those of the American underground churches, are accompanied on the guitar,[30] but more from the fact that these songs make an attempt to ask questions about the meaning of life, of technology and culture: "What is the use of all this modern technical and scientific knowledge? . . . We are merely left wandering and erring at random by ourselves, only to end by coming to the horror of emptiness and purposelessness."[31] We must certainly admit that the song quoted is a remarkable mixture of existentialism and pietism, of modern anthropological questions and mythological images. But perhaps that is just where its attraction lies.

3. *A Nuanced Critique*

It is not surprising that the majority of Christians in Russia (as indeed in the West) should be apolitical and decide to be "radishes": i.e., outwardly and officially they are red, but inwardly white. But alongside these there is a not insignificant number of Christians who reject this position. The documents available at any rate do not indicate a simple anti-Communism—just as the American underground churches do not preach blanket opposition to the establishment. On the contrary, quite early on, a clear acceptance of the Soviet Union came from the ranks of the Russian Pentecostalist movement,[32] much to the displeasure of the American Pentecostalists. Communism, said the Russians, was "no hindrance to the work of evangelism". They supported the

---

[28] M. Bourdeaux, *Religious Ferment in Russia*, pp. 64–5.
[29] S. Khudiakov, *Molodoy Kommunist* 3 (1957), pp. 118–21.
[30] *Sovetskaya Moldaviya* (15 September 1966), p. 4.
[31] Yu. Kruzhilin and N. Shatamova, *Pravda Vostoka* (Tashkent, 22 October 1966), p. 4; English in Bourdeaux, *Religious Ferment in Russia*, p. 137.
[32] Resolution proposed by G. Ponurko and I. E. Voranaev at the Second All-Ukrainian Pentecostal Congress, 1927; quoted in F. I. Fedorenko, *Sekty, ikh vera i dela* (Moscow, 1965), pp. 180–1.

social and economic basis of Communism, which was "not con-
tradictory to the teaching of our Lord".[33] These statements certainly cannot be dismissed as Soviet propaganda, even if in the
case of certain political statements—for example, in connection
with the Korean war—it was impossible to escape the impression
that this was simply a recitation of the official line.[34] On the other
hand, the *initiativniki* have criticized the basis of the Marxist
critique of religion. A first indication of such criticism is the
letter they sent to the U.N. Secretary General, U Thant,[35] in
which they gave full details of oppression and torture and asked
U Thant for help. Among the interesting features of this document is, first, the fact that these Christians turned to the Buddhist
U Thant (a parallel to the adoption of Buddhist ideas in the
American underground churches) and not to their fellow Christians in the West, still less to the Baptists and Pentecostalists of
America. Secondly, their courage is striking. They know that
their demands in part go beyond what the Russian constitution
will grant them, and therefore appeal from the Russian constitution to a higher law of humanity, and explicitly quote the "Declaration of Human Rights" ratified by the United Nations in
1960 and published in the Soviet Union on 2 November 1962.

The document shows that the *initiativniki* are not uneducated,
clumsy fanatics, although the Baptist Central Committee tries to
present them as such.[36] They emphasize in another context: "All
this is not happening in some underdeveloped colonial country,
and not under a fascist regime, but in a country where it has
already been proclaimed to all the world for fifty years that the
most just, democratic and humanitarian society has been built,
and that there is equality of all people, irrespective of race and
creed."[37]

A further indication of their knowledge of Russian constitu-
tional history is a petition dated 14 April 1965 addressed to Com-
rade L. I. Brezhnev. In this they quote the Fathers of the Russian

---

[33] *Bratskiy Vestnik* (Moscow) 4 (1947), p. 4; English in St Durasoff, *The Russian Protestants*, p. 243.
[34] *Bratskiy Vestnik* 1 (1953), pp. 4, 5.
[35] Available in English in *Religion in Communist Dominated Areas* 7/4–5, 15/29 (February 1968), pp. 1160–5.
[36] *Bratskiy Vestnik* 5 (1967).
[37] Quoted in Bourdeaux, *Religious Ferment in Russia*, p. 122.

constitution, Lenin and Bonch-Bruevich, against its modern inter
preters, a procedure which is paralleled by the appeal of the
American underground church to Jesus from his official representatives.[38]

4. A Franciscan Revolution

The underground literature which we have mentioned, of the
Orthodox, the *initiativniki* and the "latent Christians" (I use this
somewhat unfortunate term for want of a better), has already
had an effect on the official critique of religion. It has affected,
for example, the attitude to modern Protestant theology, which is
described as "one of the most impressive ideological phenomena
in contemporary Western literature".[39] H. Bräker has made an
impressive summary of the growing debate with Bultmann,
Tillich and above all Bonhoeffer, and asks in passing why those
theologians—such as the theologians of the American underground church—who are totally open not merely to atheistic
humanism, but also and not least to Marxism, or at least to the
young Marx, and allow themselves to be called "Marxists" in this
sense are not analysed in detail. Bräker suggests that the discussion of this phenomenon in Protestant theology has already begun,
but is not visible in the literature, since its publication at present
is regarded as inopportune because such a theology would give
the Soviet reader access to a Christian consciousness "in which
there no longer needs to be a clear and total contradiction between Marxism and Christianity, Marxism and religion, a model
in fact which could have some attraction for doubtful intellectuals
no longer quite so sure about 'the business of historical and dialectical materialism' ".[40]

There is no space to describe similar solidarity groups in Latin

[38] Russian in *Posev* (Frankfurt a.M.), 5 August 1966; English in *Religious
Ferment in Russia*, p. 108.
[39] V. M. Boriskin, "Krizis khristianstva i ego otrazhenie v evangeliches-
koy teologii", *Vestnik Moskovskogo Universiteta* No. 3 (VIII)/1965, p. 69;
quoted (in German) by H. Bräker, "Die religionsphilosophische Diskussion in der Sowjetunion", in U. Duchrov, *Marxismusstudien*, 6th series
("Weltreligionen und Marxismus vor der wissenschaftlich-technischen
Welt"), p. 132. All Russian quotations in full in Hollenweger, *The Pentecostals*.
[40] H. Bräker, "Die religionsphilosophische Diskussion", p. 148.

America (resulting in particular from co-operation between Pentecostalists and reforming Catholics), in Africa (for example, among the independent churches), in Asia (particularly in interreligious dialogue groups and the action groups of the Urban and Industrial Mission), in Czechoslovakia, in the German Democratic and Federal Republics, in Holland and in France.[41] They differ greatly among themselves. The best of them, however, have in common an understanding of revolution as more than anti-establishment; following the Franciscan tradition, they see their strength as lying in their solidarity with the weak and in a liturgy rooted in the art of the poor—which does not imply that it is a "poor liturgy"!

Translated by Francis McDonagh

[41] Some details in W. J. Hollenweger (Ed.), *Kirche, Benzin und Bohnensuppe. Auf den Spuren dynamischer Gemeinden* (Zürich, 1971) and Hollenweger, *Theologie in der Tagesordnung der Welt. Sequenzen und Konsequenzen* (Zürich, 1972). English translations in preparation.

Heinz Schlette

Utopian Thinking and
Real Humanity

IT SEEMS impossible that there should be anything new to think
or say on the theme of "utopia", particularly when the word
has been used here, there and everywhere, and there has been
an extensive international discussion of the theme in recent years.[1]
The connection between the series of problems specific to utopia
and futurology is obvious. It has come to the fore, especially
since the discussion kindled by Ernst Bloch's *Spirit of Utopia*
(*Geist der Utopie*, first published in 1918):[2] hardly, by reason of
the scientifico-technological predictions and extrapolations of
futurology, a chance occurrence.

Indeed, in view of all that has been written and pronounced
on the subject to date, one is not without a certain sympathy for
those unwilling to say any more about the future than that it
will be "different".[3] Our ignorance, in principle and substance,
regarding the future is in fact greater, even though we write
and say more about it than was once the case, and even though
we seem far superior to all past generations in the possibility of
foreseeing, planning and predicting.[4]

[1] See the bibliographies in *Der utopische Staat*, ed. K. J. Heinisch
(Reinbek, 1960), pp. 266–77; *Utopie. Begriff und Phänomen des Utopis-
chen*, ed. A. Neusüss (Neuwied–Berlin, 1968), pp. 449–94; *Utopias and
Utopian Thought*, ed. F. E. Manuel (New York, 1969).

[2] Revised edition of the second version of 1923: Ernst Bloch, *Gesam-
tausgabe*, Vol. 3 (Frankfurt a.M., 1964).

[3] See F. E. Manuel, Introduction to *Utopias and Utopian Thought, op.
cit.*

[4] See G. Picht, *Prognose, Utopie, Planung. Die Situation des Menschen
in der Zukunft der technischen Welt* (Stuttgart, 1967), pp. 19–32, 47–60.

This new and well-established interest in the future seems, however, to be something other than "utopian thought". The rest of this article depends to a considerable extent on one's interpretation of the terms "utopia" and "utopian thought". Although many commentators have asserted that it is useless to attempt an unambiguous and straightforward denotation of these terms, I shall not avoid a short discussion of the terminological problem, but in the following terms.

A very informative volume edited by the American historian Frank E. Manuel is entitled *Utopias and Utopian Thought*.[5] This distinction between "utopias" and "utopian thought" is necessary. When Bloch spoke of the "spirit of utopia" he made it clear, even then, that the problematics of utopia could not simply be elicited from the anticipatory descriptions of utopian literature—from Plato (as it is usually asserted[6]), by way of the utopian "novels of the commonwealth" of the sixteenth and seventeenth centuries,[7] up to the utopian or "dystopian" nightmares of the twentieth century[8]—but that only *thought about what exactly is being talked about* in this utopian literature will

---

[5] The book contains contributions from well-known American, French and Dutch authors on the history of utopia, on the relationship of utopia and politics, on utopia, natural science and technology, and on philosophico-practical interpretations of utopias.

[6] See L. Mumford's and Northrop Frye's contributions to *Utopias and Utopian Thought, op. cit.*; J. Mittelstrass, *Neuzeit und Aufklärung. Studien zur Entstehung der neuzeitlichen Wissenschaft und Philosophie* (Berlin and New York, 1970), p. 373. Picht, on the other hand, states that Plato did not want to develop a utopia but instead the "idea" of the State (*op. cit.*, pp. 33–6). This is also the view of K. Praechter, *Die Philosophie des Altertums* (Vol. 1 of Ueberweg's *Grundriss der Geschichte der Philosophie*, reprint of the twelfth edition, 1926: Darmstadt, 1961), p. 271. Nevertheless, the authors of the sixteenth- and seventeenth-century utopias constantly referred to Plato.

[7] See K. J. Heinisch in *Der utopische Staat, op. cit.*, pp. 216–65; M. Schwonke, *Vom Staatsroman zur Science-Fiction. Eine Untersuchung über Geschichte und Funktion der naturwissenschaftlich-technischen Utopie* (Stuttgart, 1957), pp. 7–16; H. Süssmuth, *Studien zur Utopie des Thomas Morus* (Münster, 1967).

[8] On the term "dystopia" or "satirical utopia", see F. E. Manuel on the psychological history of utopias in *Utopias and Utopian Thought, op. cit.* Northrop Frye, in the same volume, speaks of "satirical utopias" and "utopian satire" or parody. Mittelstrass uses the term "sceptical utopias", *op. cit.*, p. 366.

show its relation to *man* and *men*. It is possible to make this distinction more explicit in Heideggerian terms: just as Heidegger distinguishes between technology and the "essence" or "nature" of technology, which is itself not at all technical and hence cannot be left to technicians for discussion,[9] science may be distinguished from the "essence" of science, and even utopia from the "essence" of utopia. The "essence" of utopia would not then itself be something utopian, and not the theme of the authors of utopias (or dystopias), but *reflection on this "essence" of the utopian* (and on the "essence" of science), which is clearly one of the tasks of thought "pure and simple" and, in this sense, of philosophy.[10] When I use the phrase "utopian thought" (or "utopian thinking") then, in contradistinction to the utopias themselves and their historico-critical description, I wish to refer to this particular problem (which may also be raised in terms such as the "spirit" or "essence" of utopia).

In regard to the actual form of utopias or of utopian literature it is useful to distinguish two series of themes: that oriented in a scientific and technical, and that in a socio-political manner. If it is considered proper to keep the title "utopia" for the socio-political themes (for instance, there is the term "social utopia"), then scientifico-technical anticipations may be characterized as "fictions". This kind of distinction between *utopia* and *fiction* is certainly justified in terms of the thematic differences between the two types of motif, yet it does encourage a simplistic separation of the scientifico-technical and the socio-political areas; that is, in Marxist terminology, it can mean that one ignores (or minimizes) the interactions between the forces and the conditions of production.[11] For simplicity's sake I shall henceforth use the term "utopia" for both the scientifico-technical and the socio-political areas, and treat them as both comprised in the notion of "utopian thought".

*   *   *   *

[9] See Heidegger, "Die Frage nach der Technik", in *Vorträge und Aufsätze* (Pfullingen, 1954), p. 13.

[10] See Mittelstrass, *op. cit.*, pp. 371-3 (with further distinctions within utopias as draft-versions of the *Critique of Practical Reason*).

[11] The above-mentioned (n. 9) lecture of Heidegger's is characteristic evidence of the fact that it is possible wholly to ignore socio-political conditions in a treatment of technology.

Quite different prejudgments are contained in the utopias themselves: ideals are conceived, nightmare images drawn, wishes delineated, social criticisms defined, and so on. Care is devoted and attention is given to progress and the future,[12] even when the past is recalled for their sake (e.g., Atlantis—Plato, *Tim.*, 25 a, 5–8—and New Atlantis), but it is a question not of conceiving the future scientifically, but of a mode that is neither justifiable nor open to criticism in scientific terms.

In so far as the "scientific" verifiability of utopias is very slight, the modern "science-only" pundit can look on the problems raised by the utopias as already resolved—with the same detachment with which a representative of the official viewpoint in the official state Communism of Europe declares, for example: "Utopia arises only if fantasy outstrips actuality. But since we do not think beyond socialism, utopia has lost its specific function."[13] Hence utopian thought and utopias are subject to the verdict of being no more than superstition and fantasy—a judgment that is all the more oppressive when it is impossible appropriately to reflect on the historico-progressive function of positivism and scientism.[14] Whoever counters this verdict with his

[12] With reference to the utopias of the sixteenth and seventeenth centuries, Mittelstrass tries to "connect" the notions of "progress" and "utopia" so as to modify the claim to present a "best state" (as made by Thomas More in the title of his *Utopia: De optimo reipublicae statu . . .*, "Of the best state of a public weal, and of the new isle, called Utopia . . .") so that it is only a "better" state; he puts forward the following suggested definition: "Utopias are drafts that try to show how people can live together in a better way, but about which (at the time of their composition) it cannot be said whether they are realizable—or, even if they were, when it would happen" (*op. cit.*, p. 365). This approach is akin to that of Karl Mannheim, whose *Ideologie und Utopie* (first edition, 1929; third, Frankfurt, 1952; Eng. trans., *Ideology and Utopia*, London, 1936) restricts the notion of utopia to the area of realizable possibilities. See A. Neusüss, *Utopisches Bewusstsein und freischwebende Intelligenz. Zur Wissenssoziologie Karl Mannheims* (Meisenheim/Glan, 1968), pp. 112–82. According to Neusüss, Mannheim accordingly reckoned on a tendency for the utopian mode to disappear altogether (*op. cit.*, p. 181). For the opposite viewpoint, see M. Schwonke, *op. cit.*, p. 146.

[13] The view of the Leipzig Romance scholar W. Krauss, cited according to G. K. Kaltenbrunner, "Vom Sinn und Widersinn der Utopien", in *Zeitwende* 41 (1970), p. 296.

[14] See H. Lübbe, "Herrschaft und Planung. Die veränderte Rolle der Zukunft in der Gegenwart", in *Theorie und Entscheidung* (Freiburg,

conviction that utopian thought is meaningful, and that the utopias are legitimate and irreplaceable sources from which information can be obtained regarding the most elementary and real interests and needs of mankind, is faced with the full range of "proofs" which pseudo-scientists nowadays trot out against other men and especially against philosophers. In this case it is, of course, impossible to adduce "proof" in such a way—quite apart from the fact that the situation could be reversed.

Another question deserves attention at this point: I shall give a short outline of some viewpoints of the relation of "utopian thought" to the actual constitution of human existence, or, more simply, to what I call "real humanity". Has utopian thought played a part in the promotion and establishment of "real humanity"? This question in its turn needs some explanation; to avoid misunderstanding, I shall expend a few lines on a short terminological and factual discussion.

I have quite intentionally used the extremely controvertible term "real humanity". Without entering into the widespread controversies on "humanity" or even "humanism",[15] and without (in particular) discussing the fundamental and consequential question of why, precisely, in the area of Catholic theology and so-called "Catholic philosophy" there was (and, to some extent, still is) a tendency to make the words "humanity" and "humanism" redolent almost of satanism,[16] it must be said that by the phrase "real humanity" I understand a fundamental set of requirements, allegations, individual and social demands and

---

1971), pp. 62–84; M. Schwonke, *op. cit.*, pp. 91–146; and the contributions of P. B. Sears, J. M. Smith, J. R. Pierce, F. Bloch-Laine and B. de Jouvenel in *Utopias and Utopian Thought, op. cit.*; also J. Amery, "Wiederkehr des Positivismus?", in *Widersprüche* (Stuttgart, 1971), pp. 193–203.

[15] See H. R. Schlette, *Christen als Humanisten* (Munich, 1967).

[16] The reasons are to be found in the New Testament distinction between the Church or believers over here and the unbelievers or "this world" over there, and were further developed in the history of the doctrine of grace (especially the relationship between nature and grace). From the extensive literature on "humanism" I cite only: J. Maritain, *Humanisme intégral* (Paris, 1936); H. de Lubac, *Le drame de l'humanisme athée* (Paris, 1944); K. Rahner, "Christlicher Humanismus", in *Schriften zur Theologie* (Einsiedeln, 1967), pp. 239–59; E. Schillebeeckx, "Der nicht-religiöse Humanismus und der Gottesglaube", in *Gott—Kirche—Welt* (Mainz, 1970), pp. 30–61.

so on, whose realization today (that is, on the level of thinking proper to this century[17]) is requisite for the dignity of *all* persons (without regard to the diverse philosophic and religious grounds for such a "dignity"). "Real humanity" certainly does not imply in any simplistic sense the same requirements here and now for all persons in every situation in this so multiformed and differentiated world. However, it does imply (as one is entitled to assert on the basis of the principles and politico-practical considerations which led to the codification of human rights by the United Nations) food, clothing, housing and work, freedom of action, education, leisure, security, health for every individual: put more generally, and "abstractly": freedom, justice and peace in all the complexity of those demands. Consequently, it is even more true to say that the will to "real humanity", the public claim to it, the interest in and need of it, cannot be relegated to the never-never, but instead not only intend but are determined to realize its best possible manifestations in the here and now.

I am well aware that this outline of what is meant and implied in the term "real humanity" is still inadequate and far too ambiguous, yet I think I have made my basic intention clear.

The question that concerns us is: Has utopian thought contributed to the achievement or promotion of "real humanity"? It would be foolish to make this question too concretistic or to adopt the attitude of a judge. It would also be too simplistic to indicate the unresolved expectations awakened (still) by utopias and the disillusionment which has necessarily set in with so many unfulfilled wishes, dreams and hopes. Yet it would be no less simplistic to disqualify the utopias and utopian thought altogether as mere products of unenlightened fantasy and imagination.

Even if one conceded that the authors of the utopias had sub-jectively good intentions, but accused them of wishful thinking, the problem would be dismissed too lightly. I am not making a plea for immediate transference to the level of "human ontology",

---

[17] I apply this formulation despite all the problems involved in any attempt to determine the present. It is not possible to show here that (and why) we have to speak of a "reflective level of the present" which manifests the theoretical efforts and socio-cultural changes of the past.

where man is to be celebrated as a "utopian being"[18] that can only for ever articulate himself in the inspirations and documents of the "spirit of utopia". That such a human ontology, in which "utopian thought" is implied as a specific form of historical self-transcendence, cannot be excluded is a subject that I cannot examine or refute appropriately in the present context. Much less ambitiously, what I am concerned with here is merely to ask whether utopian thought has contributed to the realization of "real humanity" in and in this sense to the "humanization" of society. The question may sound pragmatic, utilitarian or even "socio-eudaemonistic", but since there is a legitimate interest in "real humanity" which is in no way injured by the pompous accusation "utilitarianism!", it is both legitimate and necessary to pose the question whether something has resulted from the utopias to the benefit of "real humanity" in as direct a way as I have undertaken in this article.

It is soon evident that the wishes, expectations and dreams of the utopias (or fictions) have been outstripped in the area of science and technology. Even when there are perspectives in utopias that have not been overtaken by the sciences (for instance, the twenty-seven-month journey to the sun which Cyrano de Bergerac described at about the midpoint of the seventeenth century, or the details of the *"voyages extraordinaires"* of G. de Foigny, Voltaire, Rétif de la Bretonne, Cabet, Jules Verne, and so on),[19] and even if one remembers that in science fiction whatever has been achieved is (quite consciously) constantly overtaken once again, it is quite certain that on the level of science and technology the relationship of utopias and utopian thought on the one side, and fulfilment and disillusionment on the other, is quite different to that on the socio-political level. Undeniably, science and technology have led to a far-reaching improvement in "everyday life",[20] and in this very way have decisively promoted "real humanity". In contradistinction to any far too simplistic polemic against science and technology (in concert with one against "positivism") praise for this achievement cannot be

[18] See J. Ortega y Gasset.
[19] Cf. M. Schwonke, *op. cit.*, pp. 16–50.
[20] This formulation was duly reassessed by H. Lefebvre in *La vie quotidienne dans le monde moderne* (Paris, 1968).

great enough. The usefulness of such applied rationality was usually quite apparent; indeed, in the eighteenth century, knowledge convertible into technicality was celebrated with a naïve belief in progress, and "utopian expectations" were often related to the progress of this technical and "civilizing" process[21]—an attitude whose relative justness is no longer a matter for dispute.[22]

But of course it would be too superficial, and too "one-dimensional", only to consider the facts and to ignore the diverse antecedent factors and later effects. Therefore I should like to make it clear that not only science and technology themselves but their anticipations in the utopias have to be counted among those theoretical (or "intellectual", or "spiritual") factors which acted in favour of "real humanity", even though the effect and mode of effect of the utopias were "indirect". If one is prepared to allow such a positive function to the utopias, then it is immediately to be conceded too that the "dialectic" of scientifico-technical progress, that is, its socio-political consequences and politico-economic prerequisites and implications, were recognized not at all, or inadequately, or too late, in the technologically oriented utopias. Indeed, one might well ask whether a disadvantage of this kind of utopia is not to be seen in the fact that when they did happen to consider the dangerous nature of the scientifico-technical process, they for the most part were able to offer only the panaceas of morality and educational theory (or of religion) as cures. In this respect, Marx's criticism of what he called "utopian socialism", that is, above all, of Fourier, St Simon, Owen and Proudhon, was not without justification[23]—even though the claim of Marx and Engels that "science" should henceforth be set in place of

---

[21] An excellent example is the plan for a gigantic Newton cenotaph by Etienne-Louis Boullée (1728–1799), the effect of which on the present-day observer might be described as that of an architectonic utopia. See *Revolutionsarchitektur. Boullée, Ledoux, Lequeu*, published by the Baden-Baden Kunsthalle in collaboration with the Institute for the Arts, Rice University, Houston (Baden-Baden, 1970).

[22] Of course the "critical theory" developed by T. W. Adorno and M. Horkheimer in the *Dialectic of Enlightenment* (New York, 1972) does not revert to a pre- or non-technical position. See G. Picht, *op. cit.*, p. 37.

[23] For an earlier allusion to this, see M. Buber, *Pfade in Utopia* (in Hebrew, 1946), in M. Buber, *Werke* I (Munich and Heidelberg, 1962), pp. 836–77, especially pp. 871 f.

the "utopistic" ideas, is clearly itself not devoid of utopian features
—whether only in the form of the conviction that the principles
of history (the "dialectic") had been "scientifically" conceived
once and for all.[24] Even the criticism of the scientifico-technical
characteristics of the "sceptical utopias" of the twentieth century
does not go beyond the mobilization of moral disarmament and
moral resistance against the tendency of science and technology
to become inhuman.

Perhaps it is possible to characterize the reciprocal relationship
of technico-scientific and socio-political utopia most proficiently
by adapting a formulation of Kant's: "The social utopia, a concept without perceptual content, is void; the technical utopia,
which is not without perceptual models, but is lacking the conceptual element which gives it historical significance, is blind."[25]
Another quotation from Jean Améry will perhaps show how an
"intellectual of the Left"[26] is able to interpret more proficiently
these difficulties basic to any consideration of utopia: "The social
utopia as supported by the principle of hope has a clear tendency
to neglect technical models and to orient itself by a pre-technical
world, one without machines or devices; the technical utopia,
which conceals the principle of *hybris*, extrapolates all available
technical possibilities of the present, wishes to liberate hope from
the possibility of disillusionment, and fearlessly turns its eyes to
a future in which man is part of an apparatus and hence himself
becomes a device. While greatly simplifying the facts (though
perhaps in this way approaching very near the truth), it may be
said that the danger of the present social utopia lies in an irrational chiliasm, whereas the threat of the technical utopia is a
form of super-rationalism taken to the point of absurdity."[27] Al-

---

[24] Cf. F. Engels, *The Development of Socialism from Utopia to Science*
(first publication, 1883); see also, I. Fetscher, *Karx Marx and Marxism*
(New York, 1971); J. Habermas, "Zwischen Philosophie und Wissenschaft: Marxismus und Kritik", in *Theorie und Praxis* (Neuwied–Berlin,
[3]1969), pp. 162–214; and E. Topitsch, "Marxismus und Gnosis", in *Sozialphilosophie zwischen Ideologie und Wissenschaft* (Neuwied–Berlin, 1961),
pp. 235–70; H. Albert, *Plädoyer für kritschen Rationalismus* (Munich,
1971).

[25] J. Améry, "Gewalt und Gefahr der Utopie", in *Widersprüche, op.
cit.*, p. 99.

[26] *Ibid.*, pp. 164–192.

[27] *Ibid.*, p. 96.

though the reciprocal interaction of technical and social utopias is rightly emphasized here, too, Améry sees just as clearly the ·dissimilarity of these two utopian perspectives when he says of the social utopia: "It lives, without any computer, without any quantitative-sociological devices and teams of statisticians, in the studies of a few thinkers, in student circles, and in a few university institutes that operate more with critical and abstract concepts than with factual material."[28] This observation should provide all the more food for thought inasmuch as the social utopias and the utopias of *practical reason* cannot reckon on a secure advance, for in regard to the area of praxis, that is, in the sense of traditional philosophy (whether ethical or political), it is true, in contradistinction to the scientifico-technical area, to say: "How one can (and ought to) live is not a question that can be answered more adequately day by day; whoever tries to answer it finds himself instead increasingly at the beginning."[29]

In the social-utopian conceptions a series of themes was always treated which concerned fundamental and persistently contemporary areas of "real humanity", as for instance, property, marriage, life in common, the nature of the State in general, religiousness, and so on. If one tries to visualize all these ideas and expectations, it soon becomes apparent that imaginary contents of the social utopias have to a considerable extent contributed to the proverbially fantastic and illusionary nature of utopian thought.

I shall refer only very summarily here to the problem of *property*. The recommendation of property held in common, which we already find in Plato,[30] and which was often supported by reference to Acts 2. 44 f. and 4. 32–37, is stressed by More and Campanella;[31] private property is quite consciously criticized as an obstacle to just politics. "Thus I do fully persuade myself", says More's Raphael Hythloday in regard to the isle of the Utopians, "that no equal and just distribution of things can be made, nor that perfect wealth shall ever be among men, unless

---

[28] *Ibid.*, pp. 98 f.
[29] J. Mittelstrass, *op. cit.*, p. 370.
[30] Cf. Plato *Pol.* III, 416 d 3–417 b 9; V, 464 b 8–e 3.
[31] Cf. Thomas More, *Utopia*, I, 7; II, 13, 15; Campanella, *Civitas Solis*, ch. 4; see also F. E. Manuel, in *Utopias and Utopian Thought*.

this property be exiled and banished. But so long as it shall continue, so long shall remain among the most and best part of men the heavy, and inevitable burden of poverty and wretchedness."[32]

The criticism of private property and the recommendation of common ownership—often connected with plans and experiments in communal living[33]—are among the main themes of the early socialists, the teaching of Marx and Engels and, for example, the Israeli kibbutz movement (the detailed differences in each case are not pertinent at the moment; I also ignore in the present context arguments and viewpoints which arise outside the utopias in theological and philosophic contexts). If one inquires into the realization of these ideas and their usefulness for "real humanity", the answer is that even if we are far from the removal of private property—whether in terms of the means of production or private (consumption and luxury) possessions (in the "socialist countries" as well, of course)—and even though there is no consensus to be obtained about the justness and advisability of an "abolition" of (private) property—then as now—it may still be said that the critique of private property found in the utopias hit a nerve point, and therefore contributed decisively to the socio-critical refinement of human consciousness, although in this respect almost everything has occurred other than as the utopias predicted.

It will possibly seem somewhat schoolmasterly after this short account of the property motif in the utopias (an account which should be taken to a greater depth and developed in terms of other motifs) to ask again exactly what is the contribution of the social utopias to the promotion of "real humanity". Is there any point in looking for such positive elements? There has been a frequent enough emphasis on the critical and corrective character of anticipatory drafts and especially of social-utopian

[32] Thomas More, *Utopia*, I, 7. See also H. Süssmuth, *Studien zur Utopie des Thomas Morus, op. cit.*, pp. 123 f.
[33] See H. Schempp, *Gemeinschaftssiedlungen auf religiöser und weltanschaulicher Grundlage* (Tübingen, 1969), especially the summary charts (pp. 299–326) and the bibliography (pp. 327–58). In this connection, Northrop Frye's remarks on the influence of monastic community on the form of quite a few utopias deserve consideration.

thought. This criticism, which derived from the utopias, is not worth attention merely because it is directed against certain contemporary conditions, but rather because of the persistence with which they applied themselves again and again to a few central themes, such as property, marriage, the constitution of the social order, and so on. In the steadfast concern with these themes, which are truly among the contents of "real humanity", we find an expression of the experience gained ever anew from "everyday life", and the insight precedent to all logic, analysis and dialectic that human life is fundamentally "disordered", but that it ought to be different and better than it is and, under certain conditions, could be. In so far as the social utopias formally contain and maintain the idea of desirable and necessary change, and apply it materially to a few central themes, they show their extreme realism[34] and their sensitivity not to "abstract" but very much to *real* humane requirements; for the *real* men are those who suffer, contend, are unhappy, who experience the "Not",[35] that which is still due, more obviously than fulfilment in the "now", in actuality, and who directly and reflexively, in a multitude of ways, bear witness to dissension and absurdity—through their wishes and longings, their work and theories, their revolts and refusals, and their prayers and curses. A consequence of this is, however, that the sum of human concerns to overcome this "Not" or at least as far as possible to control it, proves the human legitimacy of wishing and longing, which show themselves only as the reverse of that basic sadness[36] in which we become conscious of the Not. The right, indeed the human-ontological dignity of wishing, are, precisely in view of a permanently evident desolate *status quo*, to be defended against all attempts to liquidate or "expose" wishes and being able to wish—attempts that are, for

---

[34] Buber, too, speaks of the "realistic nature" of utopia—"in so far as it is philosophic" (and also of eschatology, "in so far as it is prophetic"); cf. M. Buber, *Pfade in Utopia, op. cit.*, p. 844.

[35] See Ernst Bloch, *Tübinger Einleitung in die Philosophie (Gesamtaugame*, Vol. 13; Frankfurt a.M., 1970), pp. 210–2, etc. (Eng. trans.: *Philosophy of the Future*, New York, 1970; *The Fire of the Dialectic*, New York, 1972).

[36] Cf. H. R. Schlette, "Religion und Traurigkeit", in *Einführung in das Studium der Religionen* (Freiburg, 1971), pp. 191–6.

example, just as liable to be met with among the descendants of Feuerbach as in certain tendencies in psychology.

If the quality and dignity of wishing are taken seriously, because one refuses either cynically to disregard the "Not" of this state of world and society, or "scientifically" (or, in particular, structurally) to dissuade oneself of the reality of the "Not", then one's assessment of the social utopias must be fundamentally positive. George Kateb rightly remarks: "That the real world, despite its incomprehensible variousness, still does not exhaust the possibilities of human nature is the core of utopianism."[37] Therefore utopias are to be seen as witnessing to human-ontologically necessary, socio-politically occurrent historical self-transcendence. This may seem at first to have more to do with "abstract" than with "real" humanity, yet such an impression would be superficial and deceptive. Without the ability historically to transcend, and without the special literary objectification of that ability in the utopias, men would be even more desolate and poor than they are. By means of the imaginative and imaginary prevision which characterizes utopian thinking, hope in the possibility of improving circumstances bears with it the dignity of real humanity even when it has factually no more to contribute[38] than an insistence on that aspect of the everlastingness of wishes, that is of essential dissatisfaction,[39] without which real individuals would remain condemned to frustration and despair in the midst of the various distractions of the factual world.

The constructive intentions of utopian thinking lead to basic questions of ontology and metaphysics, ethics and politics, and especially of eschatology[40] of Hebrew-Christian provenance. If

[37] G. Kateb, "Utopias and Utopianism", in The Encyclopedia of Philosophy, Vol. 8 (New York and London, 1967), p. 215.
[38] See L. Kolakowski's discussion of the quotation "Man lives not by bread alone" (Matt. 4. 4), in Geist und Ungeist christlicher Traditionen (Stuttgart, 1971), pp. 38 f.
[39] Kateb is justified in putting forward two prerequisites as the basis for any serious planned utopian society nowadays: leisure and plenty.
[40] Cf. the critical and stimulating thoughts in C. Gremmels and W. Herrmann, Vorurteil und Utopie. Zur Aufklärung der Theologie (Stuttgart, 1971), especially pp. 85–97, See also J. B. Metz, "Kirche und Welt im eschatologischen Horizont", in Zur Theologie der Welt (Mainz and Munich, 1968), pp. 75–89 (Eng. trans., Theology of the World, London, 1968).

Plato is not counted among the utopians (for which viewpoint there is much to be said[41]), then one cannot avoid the consequence that utopian thinking—precisely as "modern thought"[42] —would be impossible without the mediations of Judaeo-Christian history. This point is not raised here in order at the end to propose in a rush of second-rate triumphalism a "theology of utopia", and thus yet again to claim on behalf of Christianity something to which it is not entitled.[43] Instead it is a question of realizing that any understanding of real humanity to be put forward today can be shown to be appropriate philosophically, historically and politically, only when it is seen as a result of the process of (continuing) formal Hebraïzation in human comprehension of the world.[44] The practical consequences of this thesis in no way demand a conversion of humankind to Christianity (let alone to the Church), but the construction of a truly mature and newly critical humanism, which is conscious of its genesis, and therefore of the fact that it is conditioned, and which lives on the basis of a clear-sighted acceptance of its historical pre-formation, as it directs itself towards the future—with or even without utopias, but never again without the motive power of utopian thinking; recognizing that today only a self-critical, "enlightened utopia"[45] has any justification, and that the "unique utopia which contains all other utopias" can, in this technical world, be none other than the "utopia of world peace".[46] Picht immediately adds, however, the insight that world peace is "in the atomic age the condition for the very possibility of the technical world itself".[47]

*　　*　　*　　*

[41] See n. 6 above.

[42] Cf. G. Picht, op. cit., p. 33.

[43] In 1619, Johann Valentin Andreae could call his utopia "Christian-opolis", even though it features a practically-oriented natural science as its determinative force (cf. M. Schwonke, op. cit., pp. 11 f.); and Francis Bacon, who portrays the society of Solomon's House on the island of Bensalem as if it were a "scientific research institute" (Schwonke), has the islanders' spokesman put his question ("Are ye Christians?") to the new-comers in Spanish first of all (New Atlantis).

[44] See H. R. Schlette, "Strukturen des Christentums, philosophisch", in Aporie und Glaube. Schriften zur Philosophie und Theologie (Munich, 1970), pp. 102–22.

[45] See G. Picht, op. cit., pp. 39, 42.

[46] Ibid., p. 41.

[47] Ibid., p. 41.

Only when peace is understood not only as the opposite to war but as the opposite to *want* (a recognition that would seem to be making increasing headway in peace research[48]), can the "utopia of world peace" be prevented from losing—in the vague universality of an obviously anti-war philanthropy—its imaginative (and, in regard to the present, negative and transcendent) interest in the complete realization as soon as possible of *real* humanity—in the sense of the foregoing pages.

Translated by John Griffiths

[48] Cf., e.g., J. Galtung, "Friedensforschung", in *Friedensforschung*, ed. E. Krippendorff (Cologne and Berlin, 1968), p. 533; G. Picht, "Was heisst Friedensforschung?", in *Merkur* 25 (1971), pp. 117 f.; see also *Weltfrieden und Revolution. Neun politisch-theologische Analysen*, ed. H.-E. Bahr (Reinbek, 1968).

Maurice Cocagnac

A New Awareness in
Modern Art

BAUDELAIRE said of George Sand that she was always a moralist
but never an artist.[1] This summary judgment is a neat way of
announcing my question: How does contemporary art contribute
to the prompting of a new awareness?—If it does so at all, then
surely times have changed. Or perhaps what Baudelaire called
"morals" goes under a different name these days.

The following remarks do not represent anything like a detailed treatment of a complex and rapidly developing phenomenon which looks quite different according to the culture, race
and customs of its environment. I shall limit myself to the theatre,
although, of course, the priority I allow the live drama does not
mean that I deny the considerable value of the cinema in this
area.

Some years ago, during a convention which brought together
a number of stage people, an actor raised the question of the
origin of the "excommunication" that his profession still tends
to be subjected to. Even though the churches do not now systematically condemn the stage, there is still a certain anxiety (re-
proachful on the part of the conservative, mixed with a certain
amount of longing in the more liberal) about a free world where
the usual moral norms are no longer valid. The actor went back
to the Greek origins of tragedy and reminded us that it was
celebrated in a sacred place: on the stage the *moral* setting van-

[1] Baudelaire, "Mon cœur mis a nu", *Œuvres posthumes* (Crépet edition),
p. 101.

ishes, for the new location lies beyond the standards necessary for
any social life. On the tragic stage, incest and patricide cease to
be acts tabooed by the group and appear instead as resurgent
divine forces which are simultaneously destruction and renewal.
They take hold of human beings, who are intentionally located
on a quasi-divine level. The liberty which the tragic character
enjoys is, therefore, only a relative liberty, a freedom which only
seems so *from the audience's point of view.* In reality it is sur-
render to a number of cosmic forces—portrayed inadequately as
the pantheon of gods, but in all forms superlatively incoherent
because they remain the products of a closed, dualistic system.
Good and evil are ever at loggerheads in the world of the gods,
and human destiny often depends on a domestic row between
Jupiter and Juno.

The contemporary theatre seems intent on emphasizing pas-
sionately that the dramatic arena is a location for the experience
and discovery of liberty. It is a closed area jealous of its freedom
from any influences, whether those from below which would
weigh it down with the moral convictions of a group, or those
from a divine world above whose will resembles nothing so much
as the impulses of a supremely sadistic being.

This striving for independence is powerful enough to evoke a
number of avid responses. In the past, the very word "revolution"
was in many cases eventually identified with liberty. The revolution in the theatre will therefore appear to be a refusal to be
guided by moral injunctions, wherever they come from. Diehard
traditions, technocratic pressures, the rule of profit, the degradation of the consumer—these are so many hostile forces threaten-
ing creative liberty. The violence of criticism, police measures,
the ukases of censorship and, of course, the subtle technique of
"regeneration", help to build up a variously shaped screen of repression about all this ardent creativity.

The efforts of the contemporary theatre may be analysed in
terms of action and reaction.

*   *   *   *

For many young companies, the theatre is principally the self-
encounter of an audience. The author, the producer and the
actors are ultimately no more than intermediaries between the

unconscious ego of a group and the ego of this same group made conscious by the dramatic action. Then encounter becomes revelation. When the "living theatre" actors go among the audience during Brecht's *Antigone*, it is in order to push them to the level of moral and political awareness symbolized by the character of a woman rebelling against the laws of the city. Then the dramatic spectacle becomes a feast: not only a memorial of the past but the celebration of the present resurgence of the *spirit* that formerly resided in Sophocles. It is a feast where the man capable of play recovers his soul, and at the same time the power to communicate his soul. This rediscovery of *soul* is something that black culture has always retained and that the theatre today is trying to find once more.

This self-celebration of the spectator, with the aid of the actors, is as often as not a calling in question of his life-style. The present-day theatre is "pneumodrama" as often as it is psychodrama. Frequently it rises above psychological inadequacies in order to grasp the presence (more often the absence) of a vital spirit, a creative force which alone allows the individual to create in, by and for a group.

Of course, a great deal of contemporary theatrical experiment is either attempted demolition work or evidence of neurosis.

Satire is intentionally ferocious—even to the extent of becoming as traumatic as the reality which it hopes to evoke. I suspect that Pasolini is really an essential cannibal—how else could he so minutely reproduce all the aspects of contemporary cannibalism! His roaring frightens not only the villagers who see him emerge from the jungle, but the beasts themselves. Of course the precise fitting of style to intention that we find, for example, in Robert Wilson's last effort, is fairly unusual in modern cinema —the way to a kind of "hell, what does it matter!" is often paved with good intentions.

Contemporary theatrical experiment sometimes deliberately tries to provoke the public with the firm intention of waking it up. To this category belong all those efforts to transgress laws thought to be based on outdated taboos. Obviously it is pointless to insist on the confusions which attach to the term "taboo". On the other hand, there should be no surprise at the diversity of the efforts oriented by this viewpoint.

Scandal arrived with stage nudity. It all began with *Hair*, some of the scenes in which were ultimately only as daring as the "naughty nineties". Some other more frankly pornographic productions accord with the "voyeuristic" nature of an audience which is protected by darkness. This kind of experiment, which sometimes relies on the impulses of an often infantile audience, has considerable chance of commercial success.

On the other hand, nudity can have a quite different significance; when located, for instance, in a coherent mythology or a meaningful lyricism, it can be a "transgression" with a meaning.

We have to ask if *transgression* is not the very nerve centre of contemporary theatrical creativity. Since the answer is Yes, we can go on to ask what exactly is contemporary about it.

One often hears it said that we are living in a desacralized world. This means that we have broken with a certain sacred world which was once the cradle of our civilization. To affirm the disappearance of the sacred, however, is presumptuous. In fact, we are living in a society which is in a state of quest, and at present the surface of our earth gives evidence of very different stages in this process of evolution. There are perhaps men still living in a so-called prehistoric age. There are others who claim to be entering the era of post-industrial civilization. Of course, from the perspective of a Lévi-Strauss, ultimately a lag in progress in a spirally evolving world doesn't mean all that much. When at the same points on two very close spirals, one might well ask which one belongs to anyway. It's easy to imagine a meeting between a traditional Indian, miraculously preserved, and an electronic engineer playing at natural camping in a Californian canyon. Certain aspects of primitive culture appear in today's world. The young people dance the Jerk and can pray together only with the aid of negro spirituals. There is an astonishing coincidence of cultural cycles which nevertheless belong to different epochs. By introducing into drama a number of quasi-hypnotic techniques taken from the world of magic, producers are now relying on this very cyclical coincidence, which is tailor-made for the job of demoralizing the technocratic world with its essential dogma of uniformly accelerated linear progress. It is the very worst of transgressions to broadcast publicly opinions which are sure to upset the rhythm of progress. Theatre at present owes much to such sources as Artaud or surrealism. Harvey Cox reminds us of the need to examine seriously the number of such cultural transgressions of the morality of contemporary society.[2] A possible conclusion is that the "desacralized" society is in reality searching for a deep structure, both conscious and unconscious; theatre at present convinces us of this: by going ahead it finds *ahead of it* the inalienable values of the past.

The so-called desacralized society is also a pluralist society. The individual immersed in industrial society is no longer anything more than a collection of human fractions without a common denominator. Divided between various allegiances and affiliations, man no longer knows who will see God one day: the taxpayer, the socially insured, the professional man, the family man or the guitar player. He might easily conclude that it is the holiday-maker. For him today the theatre is no longer diversion but leisure. He rediscovers himself in the framework of a game which guides him towards his soul. It is possible for the theatre or cinema today to enable man to rediscover the fundamental freedom of his heart; in doing this he reunites what society puts asunder in order to dominate it. A total theatre can provide an awakening of consciousness, criticism of the wayward super-ego, and a discovery of responsibility without any neurotic guilt. Of course not all present efforts reach this height, but a few major successes are enough to prove that it is possible. It is enough to have experienced the production of *Orlando furioso* by a Milan company to be convinced of the possibility. Such spectacles restore to man the unity sacrificed by the progress of a demented science and technology: this is supreme recreation—the recreation longed for by an immense number of pilgrims of nothingness who are at present in the dark wilderness of the great conurbations.

This is a profoundly revolutionary transgression. Without predicting the arrival of a specific political and social form, it saps the basis of the power of the owners—a minority who can rule only by means of the unconsciousness, degradation and debasement of the masses. Of course, it can be called political in the sense of trying to formulate a way of life for the world of today.

[2] Harvey Fox, *The Feast of Fools* (Cambridge, Mass., 1969).

And of course we have to record that the contemporary theatre of spectacle looks on dogmas and churches as the worst chains on freedom. A certain number of more or less blasphemous provocations are to the point. This subject can be discussed without profit, but it can also provide food for salutary thought.

The world of the arts attack not the message of Christ but the way in which it has been used. The shock-tactics and bad taste of some attacks are excesses behind which there is something more than destructive anger.

The attack is mounted above all on a Christianity identified with a certain ethic. We must not forget that much of the movement of renewal comes from an Anglo-American world subject to the prohibitions of a sometimes insane puritanism. Hence the reaction can be as excessive as its provocation. But there is always a really fundamental refusal to identify the word of God with a specific morality. The essential Gospel rarely comes under attack, but the religion of the scribes is savaged. Obscurely perhaps, the creators of today's dramatic spectacles sense a fruitful power in the Gospel that the stratifications of more or less pagan moralities hardly allow to emerge. Their glimpses of a freer world are not accusations laid against the word of Christ, but ways to a field where it may take root and grow.

Today's theatre does not look kindly upon the established Church—least of all on any form of collusion between Church and State. The "totalitarian" Christian states and nationalist actions inspired by a so-called "Christian" faith are hardly privileged in this regard. But, here again, there is a clear desire for certain truth, and a loyalty to the essential words of Judaeo-Christian revelation: "Thou shalt not kill" ... "Judge not...".

Nowadays successes alternate with setbacks or inadequacies. This is not surprising. The world of spectacle is a world to attend to every day, not for diversion in Pascal's sense, but in order to share the impulse of truth which, in their own way, and in the absence of true liberty, certain artistic efforts help to preserve.

Translated by John Griffiths

André Astier

The Attitude of (some) Scientists and Technologists to Society

Concilium has asked me to talk about the radical doubt one finds among some American workers in research and applied science about innovations and progress in science; Paul Germain and I drew attention to this in a recent issue of *Parole et Mission*.[1] Instead of restricting myself to this subject, on which I could say no more than in the articles mentioned, I want to try to sketch a more general picture of some forms of uneasiness which can be felt among the scientists and technologists I know.

I. The Phenomena

There are many different forms of uneasiness; the reactions they provoke are equally diverse. Those which seem most typical can be listed under four headings:

— criticism of the "establishment";
— incomprehension in the face of technical development;
— a reaction against pollution and the "environment", with its corollary;
— the decline of the idea of progress.

1. *Criticism of the Establishment*

The essential evil from which our society suffers, which must be eradicated before all others, is the block produced by the fact that anyone who "arrives"—in whatever circle or at whatever level—

[1] No. 55 (20 March 1971).

always tries to maintain his position, whether consciously or not. This belief is as old as humanity. It is mentioned here because:

— in some people it takes the form of bitter and passionate hostility, capable of leading them to acts of revolutionary violence;

— its particular objects are people in established positions, in whatever group; parents, accused by their children, and of course teachers, overwhelmed by their pupils, both in secondary and higher education, just as bosses are by workers (indeed, anyone in a position of authority, any boss, is challenged by those he controls or leads, in particular union leaders, who receive rough treatment from their members.—I pass over the case of the churches in discreet silence.)

The new element is the generality and extent of the phenomenon, since the number of the bitterly hostile is far from negligible. I shall cite only a situation I know well, that of the pupils of the Ecole Polytechnique in Paris: the former pupils' association is regarded as an interest group, to such an extent that very many pupils refuse to join when they leave the college. The senior graduate of 1969 has spoken of "a complete lack of communication".[2]

But how far does this general phenomenon of criticism of the establishment constitute a disparagement or even a condemnation of technology and scientific research? *A priori*, this is hard to ascertain, but the facts are there.[3] For the most violent critics, in Europe and the U.S.A., scientific research and technology are bulwarks of the establishment, but the arguments are noticeably different in Europe and in the U.S.A.

It should be noted that scientific and technical research in the U.S.A. is financed to an important extent by the Army, which enters into contracts with research institutes. For the leader of a research team to accept a contract means selling himself to the military caste, and in particular supporting the war in Indo-China (at least at present), and so on. In some institutes, opposition is so violent that heads of laboratories, with the agreement of their entire teams, are refusing to sign any contracts with the Army,

---

[2] A collection of opinions by Pierre Marchant in *Preuves* (1971, No. 8).
[3] See the article in *Preuves* mentioned above.

even at the risk of having their research funds substantially reduced.

In Europe, although military research contracts are much less important, heads of laboratories—and professors in general—are also accused of collusion with those in power, but the terms used are necessarily less precise. Condemned are connections with "bourgeois society"; the heads of laboratories would not hold their positions without bourgeois society, and conversely society continues only because of their support. The truth of the charge is much less clear than in the U.S.A., and in any case opposition does not reach the levels of violence seen in the U.S.A. In Europe, too, scientific and technical research seems less to be condemned in itself. Nevertheless, the exasperation of young people, even "moderates", at the complacency of those who see themselves as the élite is such that they condemn at the same time (though admittedly more or less implicitly) the people who hold power, those who think they hold it, and the technology without which power would not exist.

2. Incomprehension in the Face of Technical Development

This time, criticism is not directed at men in authority or at technical research in general, but at some of the applications of research, including the most difficult and most spectacular, which seem not only to be of no benefit (to the lives of the vast majority of men) but to be without interest, to have no justification.

This phenomenon is also new, so new that it is only visible really in the most technologically developed countries; that is to say, it is plain in the U.S.A. but hardly noticeable in Europe. This would seem quite understandable: the uselessness of a task performed is felt more strongly the more one understands of the task. The question, "Why the moon?" is heard more frequently in technical and scientific circles than elsewhere. In the eyes of those who cannot understand them, spectacular technical achievements provoke a mixture of stupefaction and admiration, inarticulate but none the less real. In the eyes of experts who can appreciate the extent of the exploit the same achievements also provoke admiration, this time based on understanding, but the experts are beginning to ask whether it was "necessary". The necessity invoked here to justify such efforts can only be that of progress in scientific and technological knowledge, and in the case of the moon landings or supersonic flight the "progress", though appreciable, is no longer sufficient to justify the effort.

One of the most important results of this attitude is the dimming of the "technological flame" among the apprentice technologists of the U.S.A., the student engineers in certain institutes. News received recently from young research workers from our laboratories, at present in California, show that in the laboratories most young scientists are still working furiously with characteristic energy, and that the flame which is the strength of the United States is a long way from going out. These, however, are postgraduates.

In any case, it is notorious that certain engineering schools are witnessing the paradoxical phenomenon of boys who have chosen technology but "no longer believe in it".

3. The Reaction against Pollution

A third phenomenon, which affects very diverse groups, takes an even harder line against technical development. This is the reaction against the various forms of pollution, the nuisances and the new environment secreted by technological civilization.

I want to make it clear that I am not talking about the fashionable side of the phenomenon; of course it is the in thing to mention the environment on every occasion, at every meeting, whether scientific or theological. The problem is scientifically, technically and financially serious. The first reaction is to say that experience has shown that man, whose mission it is to dominate nature, has always been able to find a quick solution to every technical problem. He will therefore be perfectly capable of finding a way to keep the atmosphere breathable, water drinkable and everyone's surroundings pleasant. The assertions are not self-evident (and not just the last one) because the solutions are both financial and political. The case of non-polluting vehicles is well known. Because they are much more difficult to make, no manufacturer can at present think of producing them on his own unless he is willing to face commercial suicide. A solution of this problem will need a real international agreement, in practice if not in law.

I have no intention of discussing this problem at length. I simply want to draw attention to the fact that the basic assertion of "man's supremacy over nature" must be seriously re-examined,[4] not to decide whether it is true or false, but from the point of view of its conceptual content. What is nature, now that we know that men will never be able to escape from the earth? Mankind is condemned to live confined in a space the nature of which will depend more and more on the care man takes to arrange it.

The questioning of this fundamental assumption of man's supremacy over nature is also a question of the idea of progress. This is serious because this assumption does not begin with Marxism, but with Judaeo-Christian civilization; several millennia of history of an important part of mankind are being questioned in a single movement. I shall discuss in a moment the practical forms this questioning takes in various circles; not the least surprising is the appearance of religions of an Asian type in Western civilization, and in the U.S.A. in particular.

4. The Explicit (and Hasty) Condemnation of Technology

Simply for the record, I shall mention two other well-known phenomena:

— the panic shown by a considerable proportion of the population of Europe at the increasing use of information in dealing with social and economic problems;

— the condemnation of technical development as such by many representatives of the underdeveloped countries because the applications of technology implanted in their countries by the "civilized" nations often simply keep them in an underdeveloped state: that is, economic slavery.

These two phenomena are different in kind from the first three mentioned, but, even though they result from largely emotional reactions, they are important. The fact of "putting a man on a punched card"—not simply his particular physical characteristics, but his aptitudes, his whole character, even his opinions—creates a certain danger which in part justifies the panic. But should one condemn the process or the way it is used?

[4] See *Recherches et Débats*, No. 72: "La Nature, problème politique".

Should we condemn the data-processing programmes, or simply the entries?

As for the underdeveloped countries, the attitude of the rich countries to them is certainly deplorable. But it is equally certain that the problem of their survival will not be solved without technical development; here again, should not the attack be aimed at the policies of the prosperous nations rather than at technology?

In any case, whatever their merits, these two causes have been taken up by American "radicals" and the European "Left", who see in them an opportunity to justify the judgment of technical development implicit in their own condemnation of the establishment. Certainly these young people, who in their careers use modern information techniques with intelligence and success, systematically choose computer centres as the targets of their violence, rather as though these were the temples of bourgeois or technological or capitalist society (or all three at once).

II. The Motivations

These, very briefly described, are some of the preoccupations noticeable in scientific and technical circles, either produced in these circles or brought in, taken up and amplified by them.

In describing them I have tried, in each case, to indicate the causes, explicit or apparent, of the phenomena. Now I would like to try to discover some of the deeper, or at any rate less obvious, causes.

1. *The Slowing Down of Research Development*

Many questions have been asked about the real causes of the "May events" in France, and many people have seen the lack of jobs as one of the reasons for the student revolt. Without overemphasizing this factor, it is certain that the trend to the social sciences has created and is creating problems, and all the more because the problem of employment is traditionally an important part of courses in economics and sociology. The students both rejected this problem as a wholly secondary motive for their revolt (which they insisted was much more than a utilitarian or corporatist attitude), yet demanded jobs.

These facts recur today even more acutely in scientific and technical research, and form part of a chain reaction which can only reinforce the condemnation of the establishment-technology-science complex. The case of the American supersonic aircraft is typical. Whatever the real reasons for the refusal of Congress to authorize its construction (definitely economic reasons rather than its "uselessness" or the noise "nuisance"), this has meant sackings in the aircraft industry, anger among the young at the decline in jobs, a hardening of their attitude towards those in established positions who do not have to take the consequences, and a further decrease in their interest in technological problems, which will probably react on those who have the power of decision on technological projects, with the result that more will be refused authorization.

Again, it should be noted that the stridency with which young research workers demand "job security" is paradoxically all the greater where the interest of the work is repudiated. This is particularly true of fundamental scientific research, where it is well known that the rate of development has been dropping sharply in the last few years, both in the United States and in Europe.

2. Technical and Scientific Progress are low in the Scale of Values of the Young

It is very difficult to read minds. The fact of a definite disaffection among young people from technical research, the decline in enthusiasm for technology, does not necessarily mean that the value of technical progress as such is now relegated to second place. I believe, nevertheless, that this is true. On what grounds? Do we know what value has now taken over first place? The question is difficult to answer. I will examine this essential point at the end of this article. My conviction is not that of an over-zealous Christian who at the slightest sign thinks he sees a manifestation of spirituality, if not Christianity, in his neighbour's behaviour. In any case, there are very few, if any, such signs.

Paul Germain notes that certain laboratories in the U.S.A. have begun to produce machines or tools specially adapted to the needs of the developing countries. This is a sign of charitable concern, no more. During the great protest movement which shook France so violently in 1968, condemning consumer society and with it technological development, one might have thought, to hear certain slogans and see some posters (those showing Che in particular), that the movement was based on an explosion of a Latin American type of revolutionary charity. One might even have been tempted to believe in the rebirth of a young and eager Christianity. In my view there was nothing of the sort, or at least that aspect was by no means the essential one. Admittedly faith in technology dropped to a very low position, but it would be rash to claim to say what values were dominant at that time. To be more precise, it is very probable that the young people's scale of values was decapitated (their confusion supports this), and the new head was being actively and confusedly sought. It has still not been found, and this is the great unknown of to-morrow.

3. *How has Science been involved in the same Process of Con-demnation as Technology?*

Technology is a pillar of the establishment. Technology pro-duces nothing but nuisances and dehumanizing environments. But technology would not exist without scientific research. There-fore science should be condemned as much as technology.

Presented in this caricature, the argument may seem simplistic. It is not if one examines the actual connection between science and technology, not at the level of the practical interrelations of the two types of research but at the level of men's attitudes, which is the level at which the protesters make their charges—more or less explicitly and consciously.

The traditional attitude of the fundamental research worker is: you have no right to prevent me from carrying on my research because of the use others make of my findings. My hands are clean—and this is not the attitude of a Pontius Pilate, since you see me (as a man and no longer as a scientist) protest against the nuisance and destruction caused by the practical applications of my research.

To which the protesters reply: Experience proves that it is not enough to protest afterwards—it's too easy to wash your hands like that. You have to intervene at the very moment the danger arises, that is to say, at the moment when you announce your finding. In the present structure of society you have no power to do this, and what is more, you have no wish to. Given this situation, whatever value we attribute to fundamental research, we must stop it at least temporarily in order to be able to re-shape society (after destroying it).

From there to forgetting science or to making it pay for all our ills is only a short step, and one which is not far from being taken.

4. Anti-intellectualism and Anti-rationalism

Finally, with some people it looks as though the condemnation of science is the result of a more or less acknowledged anti-intellectualism.

I believe that here again the immediate origin of the phenomenon is a condemnation of the paternalism of superiors (in teaching and research), since the reproach of intellectualism brought against them is essentially a condemnation of their complacency and—much more far-reaching—of their language.

Some attitudes are very hard to tolerate because they seem to be full of contempt. No one will criticize a man for being proud of his knowledge (except someone for whom knowledge is not a value). But if he is proud of knowing more than others, that is less readily accepted; it will only be accepted if it is presented in the form of a privilege granted to him (Christians will say by God), a free gift which confers no merit on the man. If this element is missing, the resulting complacency is intolerable.

There then occurs the classic shift by which emotional rejection is followed by condemnation of the thing which provoked it. This is plain at the level of language. Talk of the "sacred fire" and "vocation" no longer works. Research and science as ideals are condemned, while the researcher's role is exalted and, following a paradox already noted, he demands security of employment. The abuse of intellectual attitudes provokes a rejection which may go so far as to condemn the intellect—active reason.

We know where such an attitude may lead. In its extreme manifestations, it appears as attempts to go back in time. It can be seen in the return of some hippies to bucolic peace or tranquil handicrafts. Or it may be the rediscovery of the collective ecstasy of the primitive Christians, singing and chanting "Jesus is coming". Or again it may take the form of a turning towards the calm spirituality of the East, a double rejection of "Western" progress and of the far too materialistic language of its religions. And then there is chemical ecstasy.... So far we have no clear evidence that students in scientific disciplines, or researchers, have reached that point; but perhaps that is the way they are thinking.

III. REMEDIES: OR RATHER, WHAT WILL HAPPEN?

In the face of these phenomena, some people, always optimistic and sure of themselves, have already found the remedies needed to bring the trouble to an end, and naturally they have already estimated the cost of the operation.

At the other extreme, there are people so terrified that their only thought is how to live during this coming period of the decay of reason and Western power, convinced that nothing more can be done.

Still others are filled with a strange hope, in spite of the chaos, because through the retreat of reason they fancy they see a new resurgence of Love.

Where is the truth? Or better, what is going to happen? No one, I think, can say. And it is possible that each of the three attitudes caricatured above contains a part of the truth.

1. *A Restoration of the Person?*

Quite a few observers, and among them many Christians, have thought they could see, and still think they can see, through the decreasing interest in technological and scientific research, signs of promise for the human person. Terrified by Michel Foucault's famous remark, "Man is an invention which the archaeology of our thought shows quite clearly to be of recent date—and perhaps to be approaching its end", they think they can find reasons here to hope. Because the consumer society, the inevitable result of technological civilization, does not secrete reasons for living at the same time as it inundates us with methods, because this lack of reasons for living is dramatically felt, and particularly by the young, the supreme value must still be somewhere else, in the person.

That is easy to say. What evidence have we for a renaissance of the "human person"? More precisely, what evidence have we that these particular words are still used, and if they are, what is their semantic content?

It is true that people still come out into the streets to protest against the war in Indo-China or to denounce the agony of the Bengalis (less noticeably). It is true that efforts are made to carry out research to help the developing countries instead of exploiting them more efficiently. But are these clear signs that the word "person" still has a precise meaning or that any ideology still exists? Isn't it a simple reflex? Is there not the uncompromising criticism of the "words employed by bourgeois society" to persuade us of the opposite?

In any case, what about the way in which the Americans deal with "technical" problems which concern man: contraception, for instance? We know[5] that often only the technical and economic aspects of the problem are taken into consideration. The ease with which the human object is reduced for the purposes of study to a few basic attitudes is disconcerting.

2. A Trend of Anti-rationalism?

The attempt to "go back in time" which we noted above (hippies, primitive types of Christianity, the practice of Oriental religions) exercises a strong influence on many people. But will these phenomena develop? In any case, are they signs of the "decay" of reason? Many other signs exist to show the "same" reason at work among those who oppose it most strongly as an instrument of the Establishment. We need only look at the way in which the many meetings of the numerous councils, committees or commissions produced by the "revolution" of 1968, are conducted to see that reason is still powerful. Only its point of application has shifted: now it is the modalities of the assemblies which are put through the sieve of an extremely close reasoning, representativeness of members, quorums, validity of votes, meaning of terms, etc.

[5] See Paul Germain's article mentioned in the first paragraph of this article.

3. *Are New Values appearing?*

It is clear that the old systems of values have been overturned. One can see that what was primary is no longer so. And those who are most "indulgent" and most attentive to the attitudes of the young can be seen trying to note the signs which will reveal the secret of what new values are at work. That is a very praise-worthy aim (and certainly infinitely preferable to condemnation pure and simple, which is the most frequent attitude). But is there any point in the attempt? There are two reasons for scepticism.

First, if we take literally what the young protesters say, there is no talk of the values which possibly inspire them, even unconsciously, because they say they have consciously and deliberately torn down all existing systems in order to start from zero. It is clear that the whole vocabulary of every form of anthropology has been methodically rejected. The young are saying that they are searching, and searching from nothing. Faced with this absolute beginning, who can say which way things will go? As one who believes that the progress of knowledge and charity are the essential values linked with man, I believe and hope that reason and love will rise tomorrow in forms I cannot foresee. But I must admit that there is no evidence to support this hope.

There is another reason which clearly destroys the attempt mentioned above. How could there be any sense in looking for the values operative among the young when the most vigorous protesters say they cannot continue their research in any form except by experimenting on the basis of a *tabula rasa*, that is, after having first destroyed the present structure of society? It is impossible, they say, to begin any new construction, even experimentally, within the present framework because we have not the freedom. You force us to begin by destroying. Don't ask us what we want to substitute, we don't know. We don't want to make the same mistakes as you. We want to try anything without prejudice. It's only by creating something that you can see the meaning and value of what has been created.

This is the gap which a certain number of young people, more or less explicitly, find themselves facing. Is it a radical doubt? No, if one means by that an explicit attitude of doubt about particular concepts such as science and technology. Yes, if the subject is "man", but take it not simply in the sense of the study of..., reflection on..., that is, anthropology, but also and above all as meaning the actual mass of the three thousand million beings who at present inhabit this tiny piece of the universe, the earth, these three thousand million and their descendants, whose fate has never raised so many questions. The riddle is all the more insoluble in that working to solve it, that is, *imagining the prospect, is to modify the prospect itself, is to create it, is to make it*. That, I think, is fundamentally the most positive aspect of the "searching" attitude of the young. And as far as that goes, let us hope that the "established men" will agree to let some experiments go on, and will help certain experiments to go on, so that the young are not reduced to destroying society first, which would definitely be a waste. I realize that waste is coextensive with, an impulse to, necessary to, evolution, but can we not do without it when evolution operates at the cultural level?

Translated by Francis McDonagh

Axel Gehring

Emancipation: A Chance of Social Freedom

THE history of philosophy can be described as a history of reflection about freedom. Plato and Aristotle, Thomas Aquinas and Erasmus, Kant, Rousseau, Hegel and the modern existentialist Sartre have shown a remarkable continuity in their thinking about the problem of freedom and dependence, of man's ability to determine his own actions and of its counterpart, their being determined by others.

The possibility of freedom is inseparably linked with that of emancipation, which is literally freedom from a situation of dependence[1] and therefore the chance to fashion one's own "life plan"[2] on the basis of one's own insights, freely and without coercion or dependence on others.

Even a superficial examination of the mechanisms of human society shows not only that coercion, dependence and mastery over others have always been present throughout the history of man, but that man has always thought about and tried to achieve emancipation. It is obvious from the number of publications that a deep interest has been taken in this problem in philosophical circles in recent years, yet it has hardly been discussed at all by sociologists, even though August Comte, the founder of modern sociology, dealt at length with the themes of freedom from coercion, dependence and lack of reason and insisted that sociologists

[1] See Ralf Dahrendorf, *Gesellschaft und Freiheit* (Munich, 1961), pp. 396 ff.
[2] This term can be traced back to the existential philosophy of Sartre.

should examine the conditions under which man could achieve emancipation.[3]

In this article, I shall try to remedy this situation to some degree by analysing the question of emancipation in the light of sociology and by investigating the extent to which it is possible for man to fashion his own actions in freedom.

I. The Plurality of Definitions

Emancipation has been defined as man's self-determination and his freedom from nature and society.[4] For Marxists, it is the need to do away for ever with man's mastery over man. On the one hand, it is not thought of as a total elimination of all authority in society, but only as a control of that authority by individuals who have become conscious of themselves as socially determined beings, in other words, as a democratization of society. On the other hand, it may be regarded as a tendency to increase the individual's role management.[5]

Despite all the differences in definition, emancipation certainly implies an extension of freedom enabling the individual to increase his opportunities and to make greater use of the possibility to live and to act on his own initiative.

This demand for emancipation is not confined simply to the twentieth century. We have only to think, for example, of Leibniz's demand for the "best of all possible worlds"; of the claim made by the philosophers of the Enlightenment that it was the task of rulers to make men free, happy and independent and that "autonomous thinking and research"[6] should set man free from coercion and dependence. As Reble has said, "the Enlightenment was intoxicated with the idea of improving man and making him mentally mature and independent by means of education".[7] Andreas Riem has defined the Enlightenment as a "need experienced by the human intellect", and has asked, in his essay of that title, the rhetorical questions: "Who can prove that

---

[3] A. Comte, *Cours de philosophie positive* (Paris, 1828–1842), *passim*.
[4] H. P. Dreitzel, *Die gesellschaftlichen Leiden und das Leiden an der Gesellschaft* (Stuttgart, 1968), p. 247.
[5] H. P. Dreitzel, *op. cit.*, p. 384.
[6] A. Reble, *Geschichte der Pädagogik* (Stuttgart, 1964), p. 128.
[7] A. Reble, *op. cit.*, p. 136.

it is blasphemous to say that the truth is harmful? Why has God given man such an abundance of intellect if it makes him unhappy? Why should it be given to him at all if he is not to use it?"[8] Finally, Wilhelm von Humboldt insisted that "according to true reason, man's only real condition is one in which . . . the individual enjoys unrestrained freedom".[9]

II. "HOMO SOCIOLOGICUS", OR OUTWARDLY DIRECTED MAN

Man's understanding of himself as a social being, *homo socialis*, who is compelled to depend on his fellow men for his life is as ancient as his demand for emancipation from coercion and dependence. Without other men, he might be able to lead a sterile, animal-like life, but not a human existence. The whole of sociological knowledge can be summed up in the single sentence, "Man is made man by man". Sociology can be justified as a science in so far as it throws light on the nature of man as a social being, in the knowledge that man is, to use the contemporary sociological phrase, orientated towards other men as an interaction partner.

Countless books and articles have been published on the primary and secondary processes of socialization, on role management and potential, on positions and behavioural tendencies and about everything that goes to make man a social being. This is connected with the conviction that man was created as a social being and with the belief that emancipation can never be freedom from one's fellow men, one's interaction partners. The question is, then, how can man exist as a social being without at the same time being exposed to the coercion that is implied in his being dependent on his fellow men, in other words, on society?

Ralf Dahrendorf has used the striking formula *homo sociologicus* to give an answer to this question and, in his book of that title, gives the following portrait of sociological man: "Let us assume that we are introduced at a party to a Dr Hans Schmidt

---

[8] A. Riem, "Aufklärung ist ein Bedürfnis des menschlichen Verstandes", in *Die Aufklärung* (ed. G. Funke) (Stuttgart, 1963), pp. 120 f.

[9] W. von Humboldt, "Der wahre Zweck des Menschen ist die höchste Bildung seiner Kräfte zu einem Ganzen", in G. Funke, *op. cit.*, p. 122.

whom we have never met before. We naturally want to know more about this new acquaintance. Who is Hans Schmidt? We can see a few answers to this question at once—Hans Schmidt is (1) a man and, what is more, he is (2) an adult man of about thirty-five. He is wearing a wedding ring, so he is (3) married. The situation in which he was introduced to us tell us a few more data—Hans Schmidt is (4) a citizen, (5) a German, (6) an inhabitant of the middle-sized town X and, because he is "Dr Schmidt", he must have received (7) an academic education. The rest has to be learnt by asking people who know both us and Hans Schmidt and they may be able to tell us that Hans Schmidt is by profession (8) a schoolmaster, that he has (9) two children and so is a father, and that (10) as a Protestant he finds life in some ways difficult in the predominantly Catholic environment of X. We may also learn from mutual acquaintances that (11) he came to X after the war as a refugee, and that he soon acquired a good reputation in the town (12) as the third President of the Y Organization of the Z Party, and (13) as the treasurer of the local football club. These acquaintances also tell us that Dr Schmidt is (14) not only a keen bridge player, but also a good one, and that he is also (15) a keen motorist, but not a very good one. His friends, colleagues and acquaintances have much more to tell us about Dr Schmidt, but our curiosity is satisfied with the information that we have already gained about him."[10]

This account of "Dr Hans Schmidt" gives us a very good impression of the multi-dimensional character of the role potential of any member of society. Behavioural expectations of the kind expressed in every role are more than a non-obligatory claim which the individual playing the role can satisfy or not. They make a stringent demand on those to whom they are directed. Man as a social being is caught in the net of his roles, the impotent victim of the behavioural expectations of the plurality of his interaction partners. The extent to which he does justice to those expectations is not left to his own discretion, because his interaction partners have a plurality of positive and of negative

[10] R. Dahrendorf, *Homo Sociologicus. Ein Versuch zur Geschichte, Bedeutung und Kritik der Kategorieder sozialen Rolle* (Cologne and Opladen, [4]1964), p. 23.

sanctions at their disposal, according to whether he behaves in conformity with the norm or not.

It is clear, then, that emancipation in the sense of freedom from relationships with other men is difficult to achieve in practice. What Dahrendorf means by his *homo sociologicus* is man in society, caught in a net of behavioural expectations and trying desperately to unravel the threads. He himself has a plurality of positions, is confronted with an equal plurality of obligatory behavioural norms, and cannot decide how he can do justice to all of them, especially when—as often happens—they compete with one another.

Dahrendorf's formula, *homo sociologicus*, like the whole of his book (subtitled "An Attempt to Provide an Outline of the History, Significance and Criticism of the Social Role") provides a very striking portrait of the characteristics of man as a social being. It cannot be denied, however, that Dahrendorf has in some ways exaggerated his pictures of man in society, whom he sees perhaps too much as a puppet, an object outwardly directed by his partners, who are able at will to determine his behaviour according to their expectations.

David Riesman created the three categories of outer-directed, inner-directed and tradition-directed man as three ideal models by which human behaviour patterns might be understood. Riesman's outer-directed man corresponds to Dahrendorf's *homo sociologicus*, whose actions are determined by others. The tradition-directed man, who follows traditionally inherited norms and value structures, is contrasted with the inner-directed individual who, Riesman claims, keeps at a distance from others and is shielded from them.[11] We must now try to discover whether the inner-directed type can become emancipated and whether it is possible here to recognize an ideal portrait of a member of society who, as a social being, is dependent on his fellow men, yet emancipated from them.

III. INFORMATION, AUTONOMY AND EMANCIPATION

When is a member of society emancipated? How is it possible to become emancipated? These are questions which have to be

[11] D. Riesman, *The Lonely Crowd* (New York, 1950).

answered. Freedom, independence, the absence of coercion and autonomy—these we associate with emancipation. How can the individual be a social being, dependent on others, and at the same time autonomous?

"Autonomy" is a term that can profitably be applied to the emancipated member of society. It is worth while examining briefly the conditions of autonomous behaviour. "Autonomous" is usually defined as independent, self-governing or living according to one's own laws, and is thus the opposite of heteronomous, dependent on different laws.

When, then, does an individual live autonomously, according to his own laws? When is he emancipated? In the first place, "according to one's own laws" does not imply anarchy. Every society has to form itself into an organized state with legally established norms for all obligatory rules of behaviour. What is also meant by "legally established", however, is that those who occupy positions of political power and are responsible for making decisions have a legal mandate for establishing norms. They must have acquired their authority to make decisions by means of a democratic election, and this always means a decision between at least two competing possibilities

The democratic organization of society is the first, minimal condition for individual autonomy, the second being information, which is in turn closely linked to the first requirement of a democratic social structure and to the third factor, the "comprehensible" political, social and economic processes. The well-informed man is the only member of society who is independent of other, heteronomous positions. The fourth condition, presupposed by the others, is a comprehensive and coherent educational system available to all.

Of these factors, however, information is the key which will most easily give us access to an understanding of the conditions governing emancipation. What are the behavioural tendencies of which the well-informed member of society is capable? As members of society, men have expectations and it is above all in the orientation, quality and form of these expectations that the degree of information, autonomy and emancipation of the individual is revealed. The expectations of the heteronomous, unemancipated member of society are usually determined by others unilaterally. They are generally of limited duration, and the member of society who experiences them almost always has only very vague ideas about how to fulfil them. He knows, for example, that "they" (the government) can do "something or other" to improve the situation of the "working man"; he is unable to express himself in more precise language than this.[12]

The autonomous, emancipated member of society, on the other hand, realizes his expectations to a very great extent on his own initiative. They are usually of long duration and go beyond the immediate and material conditions of life. The autonomous member of society usually has quite concrete ideas about how his expectations can be fulfilled, whether they are concerned with educational reform, the renewal of the tax system, or a question of international politics. He plays an active and informed part in the life of the world around him and, although to a great extent conditioned by this environment, he is also ready to condition it and capable of doing so.

IV. ORIENTATION TOWARDS OTHERS

Emancipation is, as I have stressed throughout, never a question of setting oneself free from others or of denying one's social existence. Man, as a member of society, is always dependent on others. Above all, emancipation is freedom from immature tutelage, which can only be gained by turning towards others. The emancipated member of society is the man who is orientated towards his interaction partner.

We have seen how closely connected emancipation is with information and the principal source of information is almost always the other person.[13] Our fellow man reveals the world to us in all its complexity and all its many different possibilities— his original insight into the world enables him to see the plurality

---

[12] This thesis has been discussed in detail and conclusively established in studies dealing with the sociology of elections. The farm worker is the classical example of the member of society who is badly informed and heteronomous; see S. M. Lipset, *Political Man* (New York and London, 1960).

[13] A. Gehring, "Die Geselligkeit", in *Kölner Zeitschrift für Soziologie und Sozialpsychologie* (1969, 2); *ibid.*, "Toleranz. Ein Potential sozialen Wandels", in *Stimmen der Zeit* (1970, 12), pp. 396 ff.

of objects and the complexity of events in the world differently from us.[14] He may therefore be a constant potential both of insecurity and of enrichment for me, because he conveys new information to me by interacting with me, thus increasing my potential of freedom.

The consequence of this is the paradoxical situation in which emancipation means freedom from dependence, coercion and a state of tutelage, but in which man as a social being can only gain that freedom by being oriented towards others, behaving openly towards them, and seeing in them a source of freedom.

Translated by David Smith

[14] N. Luhmann, "Soziologische Aufklärung", in *Soziale Welt* (1967, 2, 3), p. 109.

PART II
BULLETIN

Andrew M. Greeley

Contemporary American Romanticism

1. Commentary

THIS *Bulletin* has two parts: Andrew Greeley's description of contemporary American romanticism, and Gregory Baum's commentary on that description.

It is generally agreed that American intellectual life is currently going through a rather intense romantic period. Without trying to define romanticism too precisely, one can say that the most popular of the books which attempt to bridge the gap between serious scholarly work and the well-educated élites are strongly romantic in tone and emphasis. Alvin Toffler's *Future Shock*, Margaret Mead's *Culture and Commitment*, Theodore Rozak's *The Counterculture*, Charles A. Reich's *The Greening of America*, and Norman L. Brown's *Love's Body* are all books with a heavy emphasis on feeling and emotion and a disregard for the traditions of scholarly rationalism that as recently as a decade ago would have profoundly offended serious intellectuals in the United States. I shall leave to Father Baum an analysis of the broader cultural and historical trends of which the present romantic interlude is a part and content myself with three sets of statements: the reasons for the resurgence of romanticism; the positive contributions romanticism is making in American society; and the serious liabilities inherent in the present romantic revival.

1. I very much doubt that an impoverished country can afford romanticism—or at least that an impoverished country can afford a romanticism which affects the lives of hundreds of thousands of people. Furthermore, it takes a very wealthy country to make

long years of non-productivity available to its most gifted young people. American society not only tolerates but, to a considerable extent, encourages a lengthy moratorium between biological maturity and the time when it seriously expects its offspring to take on the responsibilities of adult citizens. Professor Kenneth Keniston has pointed out that the United States has managed to produce a new period in the life cycle. Somewhere between adolescence and maturity, there is a time called "youth" which runs between one's twentieth and thirtieth birthday (or, if you happen to be an ageing person such as Abbie Hoffman and Jerry Reuben, you can apparently be part of "youth" until you are forty or even fifty). During the youth period, society, one way or the other, subsidizes a long period of emotional and life-style experimentation, if not for all of its young people, at least for many, and particularly for the most intelligent and best educated members of its most affluent class.[1]

Society, then, not only subsidizes a moratorium period when its most gifted young people are permitted to experiment, but subsidizes university faculty members to provide the ideological encouragement and the emotional support and justification for the moratorium period. And the vast American consumer market provides substantial income to the various purveyors of romanticism, be it art, quasi-scholarship, popular music and even hallucinogenic drugs. Paradoxically, romanticism is a sound business investment in contemporary America. Only a very wealthy society in which large numbers of people who never have to, and never expect to, worry about where their next meal is coming from, can afford a romanticism not limited to a very small aristocratic élite. Indeed, the United States may be the first country in human history to produce not merely mass romanticism but mass-produced romanticism—and, indeed, mass-marketed romanticism.

Secondly, many of America's intellectual élites are badly disillusioned with empirical science. Students, faculty members, professionals and governmental administrators are firmly convinced that science has failed. Physical science has not prevented

---

[1] In an age when Marxism was serious instead of a dilettante activity engaged in by tenured faculty members, such young people might be described as parasites. In contemporary America, however, they are hailed by some self-proclaimed Marxists as representing the dawn of a new age.

pollution but instead produced a technology that has made pollution worse. The social sciences have not eliminated racial injustice or war and have not even provided us with much in the way of systematic understanding of human nature. The scientific approach to the humanities has deprived us of a philosophy by which we may live. Scientific methods of government have produced irresponsible bureaucracies. The Kennedy administration brought to Washington some of the most intelligent and learned members of the American professorate and it was these very men who, with all the resources their intellectual competence could bring to bear, involved the United States in a foolish war. Science, therefore, has failed; and, indeed, for some of the partisans of the romantic counter-culture such as Theodore Rozak, science is the enemy and must really be destroyed so that man can become fully man once again. Contrary to popular report, God did not die in the United States in the middle 1960s, but science may well have.

The war has, of course, made an immense contribution to the disillusionment of the American élite with rationality. The war is not merely a political and military disaster, but the symbol of the irrationality of human affairs. At the present time, American society is going through an orgy of guilt and scapegoating trying to find individuals and groups to blame for the disaster of the war. Even if victims are found for the scapegoating process, however, the war still stands as a symbol that rational, civil, liberal political democracy is apparently not able to cope with the dark, irrational, malevolent aspects of the human personality, not even when the civil society is presided over by the most rational and liberal of men. Just as pollution has proven to the minds of many Americans that science has failed, so the war proves that liberal democracy has failed.

Finally, American culture is permeated by the psychoanalytic perspective of Sigmund Freud and his successors. Even in intellectual circles it is frequently a popularized, bowdlerized version of Freudianism that has become part of the conventional wisdom, but Freud's ideas have probably pervaded the American intellectual élite as much as Marxist ideas have pervaded the intellectual élite of Europe. And Freudianism reveals the powerful demonic forces in the human personality. Having read Freud or books about Freud, it is very difficult for an American intellectual to take seriously the clear and simple world of Réné Descartes or John Locke, or even, for that matter, Woodrow Wilson, Franklin Roosevelt and John Fitzgerald Kennedy. Characteristically, the American intelligentsia has gone through another one of its periodic changes from boundless optimism to profound and tragic pessimism.

It is possible, of course, to disagree with the assertion that pollution and thermonuclear warfare prove that science has failed, that the war proves that political democracy has failed, and that Freud proves that man is not rational. One can make a fairly convincing case that technology has proved the quality of human life and that pollution can be controlled, that the war is not proof of the failure of political democracy but merely the proof of a certain style of political leadership, and that Freud has not forced us to abandon human reason but merely to recognize the constraints within which it works. Nevertheless, these counter-arguments, while they are being offered in American society, do not enjoy nearly the popularity among the intelligentsia and the near-intelligentsia of the pronouncements of the new romantics.

2. While the present writer has considerable reservations about the romantic revival, it must be admitted that it has made certain important positive contributions to American society.

(a) The American intelligentsia has rediscovered, perhaps permanently, the importance of human emotion not merely as a peripheral or residual dimension of human life but as a central phenomenon. It is mistakably clear to Americans that not by reason alone does man live and that the most rational and civilized and liberal of schemes simply do not work if they fail to consider the affective, demonic and even diabolic, dimensions of man. This discovery and rediscovery of the emotions must call into question for ever Max Weber's description of bureaucracy—at least as normative, for a bureaucracy which assumes that both the bureaucrat and the client are essentially rational creatures is not only likely to fail because of its inefficiency, but is very likely to produce a situation of collective irresponsibility where no one is responsible for the evils that an organization performs.

The romantics have also contributed to the rediscovery of the sacred, the mystical and the ecstatic dimensions of the human personality. Astrology, witchcraft, divination, Tarot cards, the I-ching, Zen Buddhism, Maher Baba, and more recently, the remarkable group called the Jesus People, have become part of the American scene. Students at technical and engineering schools rise early on Sunday morning to engage in druidic rites around sacred oak trees on the university golf course and Jesus of Nazareth turns up as the man of the week on the cover of *Time* magazine. The secularist is no longer able breezily to dismiss religion as a fading manifestation of man's primitive past. Professor Harvey Cox who, not so long ago, was celebrating the glories of the secular city is now celebrating the feast of fools while many of his Catholic admirers strive mightily to catch up.

Professor Cox's discovery of the feast of fools is an appropriate symbol of the re-emergence of the playful, the colourful, the joyous, the festive and the fantastic in American culture—a culture which in the past has been characterized more by a grim puritan dourness than it has by its ability to play and relax. Such books as Robert Neale's *in Praise of Play*, David Miller's *Gods and Games*, and Samuel Keen's *To a Dancing God* and *Apology for Wonder*, together with *Feast of Fools*, constitute a growing body of American literature on the theology of play. If, on occasion, the playfulness of this literature seems a bit forced the reason may be that festivity and fantasy are relatively new things for American Protestants.

The description of one of Professor Cox's liturgies in *Newsweek* indicates some of the style of the festivity and the fantasy of the new romantics:

> By the Jewish calendar, it was Passover; by the Orthodox calendar, it was Easter. And by the reckoning of Harvard Divinity School Prof. Harvey Cox, this congruence of holy days last week was just the right time to test his theology of fantasy, festivity and celebration. "Theology has to do more than think", says Cox. "It needs a laboratory to help us find out how to relate our thoughts to concrete action."
>
> Shortly after midnight, hundreds of students, hippies, straights, blacks, whites, artists and clergymen converged on "The Boston Tea Party", a discotheque in a converted ware-

house huddled between Fenway Park and the Massachusetts Turnpike, to participate in Cox's liturgical experiment. To loosen up, some congregants painted wall posters, others scribbled graffiti: "Free Bobby Seale" and "The Third Rail Lives". A projector flashed images of Vietnam atrocities in an updated version of the Stations of the Cross. White-clad dancers from the Harvard Divinity School mimed agony, while harsh background music boomed a dissonant Passion of Christ.

By 3 a.m., chains of dancers formed, swaying and lifting each other aloft. The crowd swelled to 1,500 and a rock band called The Apocrypha played "I Can't Get No Satisfaction". Then Cox entered, dressed in white satin vestments trimmed in pink embroidery, followed by five other clerics costumed variously in Byzantine and psychedelic robes. The Baptist minister stepped forward to an altar laden with fruit, bread and wine and read the Gospel account of Christ's resurrection. And when he finished, the silence was suddenly burst by the deafening crash of Handel's "Hallelujah" chorus.

Using the highly politicized liturgy of the Berkeley Free Church, Cox intoned the "kyrie Eleison" (Lord, have mercy), to which the crowd responded: "Right on!" Bread and wine were passed around and the congregants reacted by feeding each other. Bright balloons wafted to the low warehouse ceiling and incense sweetened the air. At 5.45, someone pointed to the patch of morning visible through the skylight and the entire crowd rushed outside, chanting, "Sun, sun, sun." "This isn't religion", complained an Irish cop assigned to enforce state laws against Sunday dances, "This is goddamned chaos."

While many Americans would agree with the reaction of the Irish policeman, they would also probably agree that the new ability of Protestant divines to engage in such behaviour probably represents a net gain for American society.

The romantic revival has also made a contribution to the willingness of the American intellectual élite to reconsider the question of cultural pluralism. While, in years gone by, lip-service was given to the notion that the various immigrant groups in American society had the right to maintain their own individual cultural heritages, in fact the assumption was that homogenization and "Americanization" were desirable and that as the uncivilized immigrant groups from Southern and Eastern Europe became more "American", they would be assimilated into the mainline of Anglo-Saxon American life. It has been very difficult, indeed, practically impossible, for the Anglo-Saxon intelligentsia to distinguish between cultural pluralism and separatism, and even now, when élites are for the first time ready to concede to American blacks the right to develop their own black cultural heritage, they persist in seeing the black consciousness as representing a form of separatism even though both the empirical evidence and the arguments of many black intellectuals clearly indicate that what the blacks are seeking is not a separate society but a cultural pluralism within the larger American society. Blacks are not asking for anything more than the Poles and Germans asked for before them—which is the right to develop their own cultural heritage within the broader culture of American society. The right, in other words, to resist complete cultural assimilation. But in the case of both the blacks and the Germans before them, American society has chosen to define this quest for pluralism as a quest for separatism, conceding a separate culture for the blacks while previously denying it to the Germans. However, some of the new romantics argue that the non-rational primordial ties of religion, race and ethnicity are extremely important to a full human life. One of the happy results of this new sympathy for ethnic diversity and pluralism is that the many impressive accomplishments of American society in coping with considerable amounts of racial, religious, nationality and geographic diversity can be sympathetically investigated and not dismissed as an unfortunate and basically transitory way to an all-too-slow assimilation process.

Finally, the new romanticism has rediscovered the importance of the primary group in human life and the immense power the primary group has over the human personality. *Gemeinschaft* did not die with the emergence of the *gesellschaft* society, and the current American romantics are not only willing to tolerate the continuance of *gemeinschaft* but vigorously seek as much *gemeinschaft* as possible in their lives—through group dynamics, experiences, communes, small informal religious groups, and similar kinds of very intense intimate relationships.

In other words, it is surely a good thing for a country when the intellectual élite realizes that emotionality, mysticism, ecstasy, the primary group, the primordial, the playful, the festive and the fantastic are part of human life. The grim, impersonal, formalized, rationalized, bureaucratized and, more recently, computerized society born through the marriage of Max Weber's Protestant ethic and the capitalistic spirit is not going to be missed. Professor Harvey Cox's Easter liturgy may well have been the funeral rite for the Protestant ethic. It will not be missed, though it remains to be seen whether another ethic can be developed which will keep a large industrial society functioning.

3. On the other hand, the romantic movement in its present form may present a number of very serious problems for American society and any other society which it may affect.

The romantics are anti-political to the point of being precious. They believe in protest or, in the case of some of the Catholic romantics, in the "liturgical gesture", but have no skills and no interest in learning the skills of everyday political organization and persuasion. They are not capable of "delivering a vote"; they are not especially interested in effecting social change through normal political process. They will not face the fundamental reality of American political life that you can't achieve your goals without winning allies. Quite the contrary, the overwhelming statistical evidence is that they have alienated those who are most likely to be potential allies. The romantics are convinced that the mass of "middle Americans" are racists, hawks and polluters. The statistical evidence is that there is a strong support in middle America for peace, for racial justice and for environmental protection but the romantics, like all romantics, have about them a bit of the snob, and while they delight in rubbing shoulders with the poor, they are terribly afraid of being contaminated by association with, much less allegiance with, the middle class.

It therefore seems to follow, as Professor Richard Goodwin has suggested, that contemporary romanticism is counter-revolutionary. According to Goodwin, even Professor Marcuse, for all his claim to be radical, in fact takes a stand that leads logically to opposition to social change, for in American society, one either accomplishes social change through the creation of political coalitions or one does not accomplish it at all. The alternative, of course, is a revolution in which a small group imposes its will on the majority, but once small groups impose their will on the majority one has not a revolution so much as a counter-revolution. Indeed, an observer such as Professor Reich, who eagerly awaits the greening of America, is in fact hoping not for reform and improvement of industrial society but for its collapse and a return to a more bucolic past—made more lively by hallucinogenic drugs.

There is a strain in American romanticism that tends to the shallow and superficial. The clever cliché and the stereotyped enemy (such as the "Establishment") appear in much romantic discourse, and the romantics have little patience for complex analysis, sophisticated planning, or elaborate organizational work. Romantics are ill-equipped to deal with the complicated social, technical and economic problems of the modern world, and are not particularly interested in acquiring competence in these areas. Social problems will be resolved by destroying the existing structure and starting over anew, and for this kind of destruction one needs no special skills. Whether skills will be required when one starts anew does not seem to be a problem that bothers the romantics very much.

While it is proper that romantics distrust pure reason, it is neither proper not fruitful for them to abandon reason completely and, on the fringes of the romantic movement, particularly its psychedelic, narcotic and violent manifestations, there is not only the non-rational but the irrational, not only the demonic but the diabolic. The glorification of the drug culture, for example, has produced not only a fair number of young Americans who live in a perpetual haze of narcotic dreams but also an extraordinarily serious heroin problem. While there is apparently no physical connection between marihuana and heroin, it is generally agreed that almost every user of heroin began with marihuana, and increasingly, it is being conceded that while there may be no physical linkage between the two, there is in many cases a psychological and sociological linkage. Heroin has been described as a form of slow suicide in which a person shoots himself in the back. The enthusiasm of the American romantic movement for hallucinogenic drugs must bear some of the burden of responsibility for the terrifying increase in heroin addiction.

While romanticism properly insists on the primal and primordial residue in human relationships, it is also frequently *prejudiced* in the strict sense of the word. A human being is judged on demographic, socio-economic, racial or sexual grounds, quite independently of who and what he is as a person. In the romantic view of things, it matters not so much who you are personally, but rather whether you are a man or woman, a black or a white, a Jew or a gentile. There are no such things as men; there are simply male chauvinists. There are no such things as white ethnics; there are simply white ethnic racists. There are no such things as policemen; there are simply "pigs". There are no such things as conservatives; there are simply squares and fat cats. This emphasis on ascriptive characteristics is frequently more important than the integration of diversity into some kind of higher unity. It is not possible for women to love men; it is rather required that women liberate themselves from male chauvinism. The romantic delights in polarization and conflict. He firmly believes in the generation gap (though there is little data to support such a belief). And he is convinced that blacks are seeking a separate society (though all the data would indicate that blacks are seeking pluralism and not separatism). He rejoices in the excesses of women's lib and ignores the fact that most American women despise the leadership of the women's lib movement. The romantic seeks out those who would destroy, and dismisses as inauthentic those who would build. And the last thing he wants to admit is that progress has occurred or that hope is reasonable.

Like every tendency in human culture, the romantic movement has both its positive and negative dimensions. Historians of the future will have to make the ultimate judgment on contemporary American romanticism. It may be that the developments of the romantic movement after the Vietnamese War will be of decisive importance.

Gregory Baum

2. Response

ANDREW GREELEY's delightful account of what he calls contemporary American romanticism is a true description, on one level, of what is taking place on this continent. The question I wish to raise is whether this level of description is deep enough. Is the present impatient search for a new culture a passing mood? Is it a romantic movement? Is it generated by certain conditions of American life and hence only as long-lived as these conditions? Or is it possibly a sign of a profound cultural crisis not only of American life but of Western society? Father Greeley does not deal with this question. He says that he leaves this to me. But if the present unrest among young people and others disaffected from society is indeed the beginning of a profound cultural crisis then it may not be the best procedure to make a list of its positive contributions and serious liabilities: for then the whole movement is significant as a preview of what will happen in Western culture on a wide scale, whether this will be its destruction or, possibly, its rebirth.

I am inclined to take the so-called romanticism (falsely so-called as we shall see) very seriously. This does not mean that I lack sympathy for the irony and annoyance reflected in some of Father Greeley's witty paragraphs. I, also, am a professor exasperated by the anti-intellectualism of some students. I agree with Greeley about the economic base of the contemporary youth culture and about the disgraceful efforts of commerce to promote and package it. I often get angry at young people because of the easy regression to tribalism, the faddish and often bizarre rituals, the sentimental religiosity, and the return to ancient superstitions such as astrology and witchcraft. I am often exasperated by the lack of political sense which makes protest actions on this continent so ineffectual and even counter-productive. None the less it seems to me that what is taking place in America is not just the creation of a counter-culture, through which young people pass on their way from high-school to responsible participation in the normative society (this is Peter Berger's view in his *Movement and Revolution*) but a significant crisis which at one and the same time challenges many presuppositions of Western culture and arises out of the deepest values of this very culture.

May I add that Andrew Greeley did not choose the word "romanticism". It was chosen for him by the editors of this volume. But the word is not used by the people who belong to the counter-culture. It is not really part of the American vocabulary at all. It is used only in its more basic adjectival form "romantic" to designate the preoccupation with love or with high ideals. But can the present counter-culture in America be called romanticism in its technical sense? I doubt it. Is a social phenomenon romantic just because it is a vehement reaction to Enlightenment culture, to the Enlightenment view of man, of the State, and of science, seeking reconciliation with aspects of human life that the rationalism of the Enlightenment overlooked or, more likely, repressed? Is Hegel romantic? Is Marxism romantic? While there are indeed authors who regard any dissension from the present order of things as either a romanticism of the Right (a nostalgic looking backward to the good old days) or a romanticism of the Left (an impatient, but equally unrealistic looking forward to the new day), this seems to me a grave oversimplification with only a thinly disguised ideological edge. I personally do not find it helpful to designate the various American attempts to create a counter-culture as romantic.

What is taking place among many people, as I see it, is a change of consciousness. A world view which, though never fully articulated, made sense to them at one time, is breaking down. People no longer know where they are. They suffer from confusion and despair. They find it increasingly difficult to express themselves in the categories of the dominant culture and they feel completely powerless to change the present order of society. This muteness and this impotence lead to outbursts of anger against society and to probing efforts to find a new language and a new style of life. Yet these efforts remain unsuccessful. A new consciousness is not created overnight. Men cannot create their own self-awareness consciously: what happens, rather, is that a new consciousness is created in them as they wrestle with new problems facing them and by doing so remake themselves and their world. New consciousness is created by prolonged involvement. For this reason, then, the people of the counter-culture express themselves in terms of a reality that does not yet exist. They hold that the only responsible language is one that does not harden the present situation into the model and test of reality, but, rather, presents the present situation as unreal, as reprehensible, as destined to be changed, as pointing to its own negation. Though the new reality does not yet exist, it enters already into the description of the present. This is exasperating to men not caught up in the counter-culture. They call it utopian.

To call the counter-culture "utopian" is, in fact, a useful designation. For, on the one hand, it is descriptive of the wide variety of phenomena presented in Father Greeley's article (including the books mentioned by him at the outset), which on the surface have very little in common, and, on the other, it is a term used by the members of the counter-culture themselves. To be utopian means to be possessed by a higher vision and thus refuse to accept the present as real.

What is characteristic of the contemporary upheaval in America—a point perhaps not sufficiently brought out by Father Greeley—is its radicalism. By radicalism I simply mean that the solution of every problem begins with the negation of the present state of affairs. The present must be destroyed before we can discover which way to move. This element of negation is often infuriating; it can lead to injustices, to repetitive conversations, to useless slogans and clichés. What is the root of this radicalism in the U.S.A.? It is not the dialectical tradition of Hegel and Marx! It is, rather, intimately connected with the central political problem of American society, more crucial than monopoly capitalism and economic colonialism, namely the massive presence of an underprivileged race, the negroes. The U.S.A. is

marked with this problem as by a paint brush; it is visible everywhere. One cannot turn away from it. First the black people
themselves, and then white Americans through them, have discovered that the land of the free, the ideal democracy, the country
of equal opportunity, is for the black man a land of bondage.
Americans have discovered that their solemn founding documents, guaranteeing the rights and freedoms of every citizen,
were not intended, by their authors, to apply to the slaves who
had been imported from Africa. The oppression of the black
is so deeply woven into the institutions of America and hence
into the consciousness of its people that it is almost impossible
for the ordinary good person of common sense to discover it.
We have here a classical example of false consciousness. The
situation of the negro can only be discovered by the person who
is ready to invert the categories in which he has understood his
national existence. Only through negation is truth available.
America must be acknowledged in the jargon of the radicals,
as Amerika—the spelling is taken from Kafka's novel. The
true America can become a reality only as this negation is
taken seriously.

The race problem in the U.S.A. anticipates a problem that
will become universal on this globe. This is not the place to show
how the hegemony the white man has achieved—through Renaissance, Enlightenment, the scientific revolution and the ideal of
a rational society—has led to the Westernization of humanity,
and hence in some sense to the servitude of other races. It is
painful to think of the convulsions ahead of our culture as we
come to see, or refuse to see, our involvement in the servitude of
men! In the U.S.A. this conflict is anticipated, and to the praise
and honour of the American people it must be said that no other
country in the world has ever, to my knowledge, permitted such
a conflict to become so vocal and so visible.

The racial problem, if I may use this euphemism, is a crucial
dimension of American Life. It is the social justification of radical thought! For the members of the counter-culture the situation of the black has become the model for the understanding of
the entire social reality.

Radicalism is more deeply associated with the American tradition than is usually acknowledged. No one in America has shown

as well as Rosemary Ruether, in her book *The Radical Kingdom*, how closely linked the Western radical tradition is with the so-called radical wing of the Reformation in the sixteenth century, and how influential this wing has been in the creation of American Christianity. The various sixteenth-century groups of anabaptists and spirituals (whom traditional history books have largely neglected) condemned the institutions of Church and State as the source of evil in the world. Church and State were so profoundly corrupted by sin that they were beyond reform. The anabaptists and spirituals also denied the traditional doctrine of original sin. This doctrine robbed the ordinary person of confidence in himself and hence gave more power to the institutions. Man was good, the radicals held, because the spirit was with him. The evil in the world was due to the system. While the entire radical wing of sixteenth-century Christianity negated the established institutions, they reacted differently to them, some violently, understanding their action as God's judgment present in history, others by dropping out and moving to the margin of society, others again—and these were to survive in later centuries—by founding utopian communes in which the love of God's kingdom was to be anticipated. Yet while they chose different ways of reacting, they all expressed their views of the world in the same apocalyptical language of Scripture. They saw the world under an imminent divine judgment, punitively present in the evil that befell society, and graciously present in the building of their own community. Rosemary Ruether shows that the entire revolutionary language of the West was derived from Christian radicalism and ultimately from apocalypticism.

The utopian, radical form of Christianity has profoundly influenced American religion. Some of the early communes have survived in the U.S.A. What is more important is that Americans developed a self-understanding in terms of the apocalyptical categories; they were the chosen people, God had saved them from the Land of Oppression (Europe) and established them in the Promised Land. America was God's own country, the defender of God in history, and its enemies were satanic powers. Today the radicals have adopted the same apocalyptic images, except in reverse: America now is Amerika, the imperialist exploiter of the world. Rosemary Ruether rightly insists that the radical tradition of the New Left in America is not derived from Marxist thought and experience but from the apocalyptic and utopian trends of American religion.

The present upheaval in American society may also be understood as a crisis of schools. After all, the schools on various levels are the institutions by which modern society perpetuates itself. They are in a certain sense the novitiate of Western culture. It is not surprising that at times when this culture is radically questioned, these schools come under fire.

Over the last ten years a vast amount of literature has been created in the U.S.A. on the ills of the educational system and the universities, from radical reforms of the learning processes to radical negations of schools altogether (Paul Goodman, Ivan Illich). What is the kind of person the schools produce? What kind of culture do they perpetuate? Quite independently from the content of the teaching, how does the school as process affect the young people who attend it? What is widely objected to is the authoritarian structure of the school system, evident in the very architecture of the classroom: namely, that there is one man who knows the truth and teaches it from his elevated chair and others who are learning this truth from him and who sit quietly facing him. While this system creates passivity and the spirit of conformity in the students, it generates a false idea of objective truth in the teacher. The search for and the communication of truth thus demand detachment and value-neutrality. It is not difficult for the radical critics to discover the ideal of society secretly built into the system of education and to reveal the ideological use of science and its institutions.

According to the American genius, debates never remain in the abstract. The criticism of schools and universities has led to the creation of experimental schools, some of which fail after short periods, and to many experimental programmes at universities. It has led to a critical review of the sources of income of schools and universities, and often to the discovery that some science departments, for the sake of large sums of money, direct most of their research to the war effort, and that other institutions are financed by people or groups dedicated to the defence of the *status quo*. The supporters of the institutions of learning, in turn, have begun to look into the spirit that pervades among faculty and students, and there are many institutions, including Protestant seminaries, that have been cut off from funds and had to close their doors or drastically limit their scope.

May I add, especially for the European reader, that while positivism and behaviourism are widespread in American universities at the present, they are not "typically American". The critique of positivism and behaviourism which accompanies and grounds the present criticism of the university can base itself on an American philosophical tradition critical of the subject-object model of truth, on which Enlightenment science was built. The American pragmatism of Peirce, Dewey and James has always regarded reality as an unfinished process, in which truth is not the conceptual conformity of a finished subject to the finished world that is known by him, but as a more complex action of the mind, by which the subject builds himself as well as the world which he knows. Knowledge of the important things is always costly because the knower must be willing to be changed and to change the world. (For the interest of the German New Left in American pragmatism, see J. Habermas, *Erkenntnis und Interesse*.)

While the angry students are usually quite unable to articulate their critique of the university—and all too often not committed to such an intellectual endeavour—they have none the less sensed the Achilles' heel of Enlightenment science. No lamenting of administration and faculty will be able to prevent the approaching crisis of science in regard to methods, orientation and models of truth.

Another aspect of the American counter-culture, one to which I attach great importance, is the protest against the rationalistic understanding of man. In depicting the positive contributions Father Greeley has presented a good picture of what is in fact taking place among the young people. The counter-culture protests against the split between knowledge and feeling that is deeply rooted in Western culture and embodied in the institutions we have inherited. Regarding reason as the highest faculty and looking down upon the other faculties as inferior, we have become estranged from our feelings, our sexuality, even our body. They have become strangers to us and sometimes even our enemies, whom we must manipulate through intelligence and will power. The protest of the counter-culture against this impoverishment is again so deeply marked by utopian radicalism that it usually begins with the negation of the present and simply celebrates irrationalism. This is how I interpret the new interest in the absurd, the drug culture, the preoccupation with exotic religions and occult practices, and much of what is patently bizarre in the behaviour of the youth movement.

In this concern for human wholeness the counter-culture is allied with the psychotherapeutic movement widely spread in American culture, i.e., with the systematic attempts, through reflection, conversation, confrontation, and various other techniques, to acquire a new awareness of the emotional life, to wrestle with the roots of illness often hidden from consciousness, and to repossess the body not as an obedient instrument of the mind but as a sensitive mode of being in the world.

Here, too, we have the anticipation of a profound cultural crisis. In the eyes of the counter-culture it is, curiously enough, not the priesthood but the medical profession that is most guilty in promoting the separation between body and soul. The medical establishment has become problematic to members of the psychotherapeutic movement as well. In medicine, man is looked upon almost exclusively in biological terms. The body is the object of medical practice. The entire medical system has become objectified, impersonal, overly specialized, and into the bargain excessively expensive. It is often quite unable to help great numbers of people in their suffering. But is it really true that you have to be a medical doctor to heal? Is it not possible to draw more sensitive, therapeutically gifted people into the work of healing and introduce them to work in conjunction with medical doctors? Are we not in need of healers who instead of having an objective knowledge of human biology, are deeply in touch with their own bodies, healers who sense how the emotional life blocks and releases their own bodily energies, and who are able to communicate to the sick a new confidence in regard to their bodies and a new sensitivity to the voice of their illness?

In my view, then, the utopian radicals in the U.S.A., despite the diverse and often self-contradictory forms of their protest, are a symptom of a profound cultural crisis of Western society.

They anticipate conflict and upheavals that will spread in other parts of the world.

What is my own reaction to the counter-culture? While I regard the utopian spirit as dangerous, while I think that utopianism often makes people unrealistic in their hopes and thus leads them ultimately to despair, while I think that utopianism often makes people see the world in black and white, divides humanity into "we" and "they", inserts contempt in the very effort to change society and thus easily ends up in a paranoid vision of the world, while I think that utopianism leads to unrealistic political action and the loss of political sense that Father Greeley rightly laments, I still hold that there is no other way of overcoming the present than by an imaginative critical representation of the future that does not yet exist. Instead of rejecting the utopian trend, we must search for a critique of the imagination. We must find principles or methods by which we might distinguish a fantasy which ultimately intensifies man's alienation, from the imagination which presents him with new possibilities of being himself. Instead of rejecting the utopias of our young people, we must undertake a constructive critique of their utopias as the only way, possibly, of facing the cultural crisis coming upon the West.

PART III
DOCUMENTATION
CONCILIUM

Ernst-Otto Czempiel/Heinz-Theo Risse

Peace Research

THIS article is an attempt to sketch a systematic notion of peace research. It is divided into three sections: the concept of peace and the general orientation of peace research; the main areas of research; the main emphases.

I. CONCEPT OF PEACE

Even though it is at present unnecessary to offer a precise definition of the term "peace", a provisional acceptation in regard to the objects and general goal of peace research is requisite. In this sense peace may be defined as a continuous pattern of processes in the international system, having three reciprocally effective characteristics: an assured absence of the organized human use of force (war); an ongoing reduction of the structural element of force in the control of conflicts; a simultaneous increase of opportunities for individual development and freedom, and for social development. This comparatively simple definition has several advantages. It is neither so formal nor so complicated (and therefore almost unrestricted) as other models. It is not confined to "negative" peace, and does not employ a chiliastic positive concept of peace which, when fully realized, could lead to a renewed legitimation of the use of force. It therefore avoids the danger of pacification and that of revolution (in the traditional sense of this term). It aims at continuous progress in the system as in its components, without denying that progress by permitting the organized use of force.

This definition also enables peace research to be demarcated proficiently in view of its objectives and in regard to other social-scientific and political-scientific disciplines. In this perspective "peace" is an international and not a national state. It refers to systemic and not national conditions. Admittedly the international system consists of nations, and to that extent there is a close connection between their states and the state of the system. However, this relationship is to be conceived neither as a simple cause-result relationship nor analogously to a living organism. The system state is more than the sum of its component states; the reciprocal effects produce more than a new quality of the system state which is to be apprehended as such. On the other hand they do not comprise all internal states of the system components, but only a part, which may be defined more specifically: those internal states which exert at least an hypothetical influence on the system behaviour of the nation or group of nations. The same applies to peace as an object of peace research, to peace research, and to the aspect of progress to be sought under the title of peace. The societal circumstances of the system components need be influenced only to the extent that ensures a system behaviour in the appropriate social units which produces (or makes possible) non-violent (or increasingly non-violent) solutions to conflicts. This extent should be conceived not as a limit and a goal, but as an intermediate stage, a starting-point and a threshold, progress beyond which begins at a higher level of international intercourse.

We are not to understand peace research as an intention to improve the foreign or international situation. Nevertheless, such intentions are neither dispensable nor illegitimate. For example, it is important to study the foreign policies of political parties, the possibilities of arms control and disarmament, nation-building strategies, foreign economic policies, or the Vietnam war in international law. But these analyses cannot simply be included under the goal of peace, and can be thought of as peace objectives only if the goal of peace is conceived as vaguely as in traditional political rhetoric. The demand for such analyses should be addressed to the appropriate scientific disciplines and not solely to peace research.

The notion of "peace relevant" research is not to be affirmed in contradistinction to peace research. This concept is invoked to promote progressive studies which could not otherwise be directly associated with peace. But this goal is better served by a terminology which makes more precise distinctions.

Positively formulated, peace research would, in our understanding, have to concentrate on an elevation of the modes of conflict solution in the international system to an (in principle, and hence historically assured) higher stage, and on an examination of the conditions, opportunities and strategies requisite to this end. This allows concentration on the major problem: the removal of the "Hobbesian situation" in which States move like gladiators in a quasi-lawless area, basing themselves on the assumption that man is naturally an enemy to man. Of course some decades of international co-operation and large-scale research will probably be necessary before any real results are achieved.

1. *Formal Characteristics*

Peace research studies systemic processes and interactions. It does not have to examine entire national systems; it is frequently compelled to make do with parts of such a system, or even with mere bipolar relations. It is decisive that foreign policy does not become a research object as the foreign policy of the nation or of nations, or even as the foreign political ideas of parties and groups. Foreign policy is comprised in peace research only as an element of systemic relations, hence only in so far as it influences the system permanently and structurally. What is in question is the conventionalized, quasi-habitual conflict behaviour of the social unit, and not the actual foreign-political decision.

On the other hand, the internal states and conditions of the system components must be comprehended in so far as they determine this conflict behaviour. The problem of revolution, for example, is excluded since it is primarily a change in an internal societal order.

Therefore peace research is a research into bases. It aims at systematic results which should allow reliable predictions. It is not primarily a question of approaches to rational foreign political activity directed towards peace, but of an elucidation of the (for a long time) largely irrational area in which foreign and internal politics are played out. Only one area of direct, practical application is immediately in question: disarmament.

In this kind of basic research theory and practice are applied so that commitment to peace is not excluded and the requirements of scientific methodology are not neglected in favour of this commitment. Practice as political decision is separate from theory, but only in order that theory and the scientific quality of its results may be the more precisely narrowed down.

2. Content

Peace research is directed less towards specific static formal patterns of the international system than to the processes or modes of conflict regulation. The actual political shape of peace therefore remains open; it depends on the historico-regional and socio-economic and technological conditions. The question of a world-state remains just as open as that of the possible preliminary stages. These mid-term and long-term formal patterns are chronologically far too distant to be open to meaningful discussion. For instance, as far as the peace research of West Germany is concerned, the form of the African sub-system (as a regional system) is only peripheral, whereas this is not true of the shape of the North-South system (or parts of it), to say nothing of the East-West system—which for the Federal Republic is a primary object of peace research. The level of conflict regulation is the decisive factor. The actual form of the system is affected only if a specific level has already been reached, say in West Europe or in the Atlantic system. Since any further progress is not absolutely possible if the open system (the system of non-associated national-State units) is retained, a change in it becomes a precondition for further development.

Likewise peace research cannot simply be identified with the goals of a unit. It is oriented to the development and application of an increasingly non-violent mode of control which applies to all conflict partners. The societal and political order of the system components is not comprised in this research under general and/or ideological but only functional aspects: its local value for the behaviour and state of the system is to the fore. The study of dominative, social and scientific orders must indicate their structural significance for a more peaceful form of system behaviour.

The connection of the contents and vehicles of justice with peace is one of the fundamental problems of peace research. The claim of justice in the past as in the present has nevertheless often served to legitimate the use of force. The notion of justice in an open system, its quality, its confirmation, its claims and the possibilities for its realization therefore become important questions of peace research. In the secular sense they already appear in the notion of "structural force", but—theoretically and strategically —are inadequately differentiated. The dilemma of chiliasm and that of the just war must be avoided, and an innovative theory developed in their place to indicate the bearers of just claims in the system, i.e., to decide whether it is still possible for States— and if so, under what conditions—to raise claims of that nature, or whether individual men and certain groups are not bearers of claims to right which precede the traditional claims of States. The concept of the State could be de-hypostatized, and its claim to obedience demythologized. This would also affect its relations to other States considerably. For example: the goal of "German re-unification" would become irrelevant in regard to the goal of improvement of the political and economic standard of life of individuals in the German Democratic Republic.

Peace research is necessarily concerned with a new understanding of foreign politics. As a result of still basically monarchistic concepts of the State, the understanding accepted hitherto is oriented to anonymous group values, which it attempts as far as possible to interpret and apply. A new understanding would have to introduce the social individual as the central reference unit, and to degrade group boundaries to a function of individual needs. The effect on the significance of territorial boundaries would be significant. In this understanding the external group would be conceived as a possible internal group, and the relationship to it adjusted correspondingly. If and in so far as the sum of social conditions and states was understood under "common good", i.e., those which serve the individual and his family in regard to optimal chances of freedom and development, there would also be a connection with peace. Any other understanding which envisages an anonymous universal interest is inimical to the goal of peace as understood here.

Such a change in the evaluation of the functions of a social unit represents an extremely difficult but extraordinarily important goal. Even though it cannot be taken for granted that theoretical work in this area will have immediate political results, the change in terminology and therefore in the conceptual world would be a considerable advance. The approach of peace research itself has to be seen as a still inarticulate foretaste of such a concept of foreign and international politics.

Peace research does not develop a strategy to achieve the aims of one side. This means that almost the entire range of military strategy is dispensed with. It is also impermissible to possess and to develop such strategies. They are partly responsible for the relative stability of the system of reciprocal fear. But the latter is also —hence its dangerous ambivalence—a specific variant of traditional behaviour patterns (though—by virtue of an incredible destructive potential—a highly refined variant) which remain directed to the maximal power and profit of either one or the other side and do not in principle exclude the use of force, even if the partners of the threat system mutually control this accretion of power, dispense with the use of force and try to discipline the instruments of force. Therefore, peace research is not just any kind of strategy research. Its strategic goal has instead to be the development of foreign-political modes of behaviour, which effect an increasingly non-violent system behaviour of social units. In addition, strategies have to be developed which can motivate and stimulate one's own as well as other social units' social learning.

II. Areas of Peace Research

Peace research may be roughly divided into the analysis of conflicts and conceptual accounts of solutions of those conflicts.

1. Analysis of Conflicts

Conflict potentials can be expected on four levels: the system and its conditions and processes; foreign politics; internal politics and its social structures; processes connecting the three foregoing levels.

On the systemic level, conflict conditions are to be distinguished from conflict processes. Conditions for conflicts which have to be understood and analysed are: the level of technology and its consequences for the possibilities and density of communication and interdependence. Even in this light the diverse sub-systems of the universal international system are to be strictly distinguished one from the other. The conflict conditions which give rise to the African sub-system are *in principle* other than those of, say, the European sub-system.

By reasons of repeated actions and the complexity and permanence of their practice, confirmed and (therefore not easily changed) processes also count as conditions. In addition there are the currents of information, capital and trade. Such a conflict potential is formed by, say, the import restrictions imposed by the industrial nations, or by the fact that the shipping lanes are traditionally controlled by a few companies.

Finally we have to include among systemic conflict conditions the historical experiences of the system members, their behavioural traditions and their conflicting cultures. Conflict is not a constant but a dependent variable. The image it has developed in modern Europe dominates at the moment, but should not obscure the fact that it has taken other forms and can take others in the future.

These conditions form the basis of the particular systemic processes—the interactions which constitute the conflict. Their collective nature distinguishes them from the conflict actions, or foreign politics. Systemic processes (synonymous with international politics) are formed by the foreign policies of the system members under the specific conditions of their interaction. A distinction may be made between three classes of such processes. First there are those provoked by aggression: one or more system members pursue goals which can be satisfied only at the cost of the other system members, whether these goals are ideological, economic, political or territorial. Conflict processes of this kind occur relatively seldom. More frequent are those which arise from divergent interests, that is, from the—initially unintentional —incompatibility of economic or political interests. The third class of processes arises from pure interaction: that is, from the fact of acting together. It is hypothetically frequent. This group at present comprises much of the armaments race. It has lost its references and tension and is largely an almost automatic course of interaction. Conflict elements in interaction can also arise from faulty diplomatic know-how, from communications problems and from social distance. Increasing interdependence is also a source of conflict potentials.

On the level of foreign politics there are independent goals of the unit in question as well as their reactions on the interactions— in the foreign-political decision apparatus, the political élite and the administration. It is important to study to what extent foreign-political decision processes feature aggressive goals or interests, and a degree of exclusiveness which makes their collision with others unavoidable, or avoidable only with difficulty. The perceptiveness of the decision-makers, their images of conflict, and the structure and training of the diplomatic service must be taken into consideration. The ends-means complex formed in the decision process (right up to the choice of instruments) must be studied. The flow of decision itself has to be analysed.

The level of foreign politics is closely related to that of internal politics, which may count as its condition. We have to ask which socio-political formations of a unit are relevant to its external behaviour or the decision process which produces a specific foreign policy. The object of primary analysis here is the socio-economic dominative system of the units as the releaser or promoter of aggressive aims or manifest external interests. Cultural and societal behavioural norms, the degree of domination, and inner-social aggression and frustration potentials must also be ascertained. The educational and legal systems must be examined to see whether and how far the forms of socialization they give rise to promote specific forms of conflict behaviour and resolution. The adaptive and learning capacity of a society must be included in research because of the significance which auto- and hetero-stereotypes can have for foreign-political conflict behaviour.

These three levels of conflict can be isolated with relative ease. In the process, however, political reality is distorted, for practice concerns all three levels. For example, conflicts arising from divergent class interests concern system conditions, system processes, foreign-political decisions and inner-societal interests. One of the most difficult theoretical and practical problems is to determine the share of the various levels in causation. The level at which one starts is not so important; but the specification of the "linkage" is decisive. It alone makes possible an exact analysis of the dispositions of the conflict, which in its turn is requisite for a meaningful solution.

2. Concepts of Conflict Resolutions

The development of conflict resolution strategies can begin with artificially posited or hypothetical conflict bases (say, the East–West conflict, or the social differences between the U.S.A. and the E.E.C.).

Aggressive-type conflicts always, and divergent-type conflicts sometimes, require an alteration in societal circumstances. For example, a resolution of black-white conflict in South Africa is inconceivable without a shift in the social norms of the élite in the Republic of South Africa and without an improvement in their sensibility, and so on. What possibilities are there of promoting such a development? Or what constellations in bourgeois republics influence the reproduction of armaments, and how can this hypothetical "industrial-military complex" be run down? How can the hypothetical "ideological-military complex" in the socialist countries be influenced? How can the Federal Republic influence the dictatorships in Greece and Spain or the government of the Democratic Republic? What social formations must be changed in East and West in order to allow a co-operative structure to emerge from the cold war situation? What instruments do we possess to allow such a process of corrective control?

III. POSSIBLE EMPHASES OF PEACE RESEARCH

1. Analysis

The following are groups of themes on the *system* level:

(a) The problem of right and justice in the international system. The vehicles and claims must be redefined, and the systemic direction of peace redetermined.

(b) The socio-ideological antagonism between socialism and capitalism and the opportunities for co-operation.

(c) The barriers to West European integration and their foundation in the economic and political spheres.

(d) Between sovereignty and integration: a new order for the European system (the model of the European order of peace); cf. (b) above.

(*e*) Division of labour and leadership: the future of the Atlantic system.

(*f*) Communications systems, information channels and tension. The relationship between language barriers and conflict.

(*g*) The development problem as a divergence of interests between industrial States and developing countries. The interests of the developing countries have to be set against the achievements of the industrial nations, and the development function of these achievements discussed. The commitment to development aid must be converted into terms of precise political formulas and its extent defined more exactly.

(*h*) The armament-disarmament system. This is at many points identical with the foundations of the East–West conflict. Armament must be examined as an independent as well as a dependent variable. This is precisely the point at which systemic and national conflict potentials converge.

The following are groups occurring on the foreign-policy level:

(*i*) Tension factors in the foreign-policy decision processes of diverse units.

(*j*) Democracy and foreign policy.

(*k*) Education, information, and perceptual structures of foreign-political élites.

(*l*) Socio-historical traditions of external behaviour. Here it is necessary to study diverse ends-means complexes as they are mediated socio-administratively, and to see how far they contain stereotyped tension elements.

(*m*) Foreign-political tension and mobilization of inner-political consensus. Foreign politics is often used as an instrument to secure a non-stable form of rule or even merely to make a consensus easier to obtain—when framing a budget, for example. These connections have to be analysed so that the actual existent foreign political conflict situation can be adequately assessed.

(*n*) The analysis and classification of foreign-political objectives of different units. It is necessary to distinguish aggressions and divergences of interests in the system-input.

Thematic groups in the area of *internal politics* and *societal structures*:

(o) Dominative systems and foreign politics. Agreement on the preferred means of internal and external conflict resolution.

(p) Social order and foreign policy. The flexibility of the social structure, possibilities of removal of any internal conflict, readiness to adapt and speed of adaptation (readiness for external conflict as the result of internal frustration), together with the stratification of society and income distribution in a society (conflict readiness of the underprivileged) must also be studied.

(q) The educational system and foreign politics. Which conflict and conflict-solution norms are socialized in the educational system, and which friend-foe stereotypes and prejudices does it feature?

(r) Which larger groups and interests determine external political interests? Here the main heads for investigations are, e.g.: economic politics and foreign politics, parties and foreign policies, the armed forces and foreign politics. Again it is not a question of descriptive investigations but of analyses of conventionalized conflict-oriented patterns. It is a question of research into the bases, not of historiography.

(s) Ideology and foreign politics. How do ideological objectives relate to external objectives?

(t) The self-understanding of society and foreign politics. This complex refers to the above-mentioned new concept of foreign politics. What has to be analysed is the basic orientation of a society either to expansion or to progress (in the sense of an increased chance of individual development). In this way it is possible to prevent a largely compensatory system-input changing poles under the aspect of efficient foreign politics.

In regard to the conjunction of levels the following is of basic importance:

(u) For example, the East–West conflict has to be investigated on the systemic level (conflict traditions, constellation traditions, aggressions, divergences, interactions, security dilemma), on the level of the foreign politics of system members (internally conditioned tension factors, faulty perceptions, mobilization of consensus, etc.), and on the level of internal politics (interests of economic, party and military groups, conflict readiness and behavioural traditions of the system members). This must occur simultaneously or in a systematic order. Otherwise the isolation of individual factors and the faulty evaluation of conflict systems are unavoidable and the attempt at conflict resolution is doomed from the start. The conjunction of the different levels is best treated by team work and interdisciplinary co-operation—encouragement of which is one of the most important tasks of an organization for promoting peace research.

2. Concepts of Conflict Resolutions

Because of the novelty of the problem there are no major problematic emphases to single out here. Even the least evidence of progress is desirable and urgently required. The following are among the most urgent areas:

(*a*) Tension-reductive strategies.

(*b*) Strategies to remove the reservoir of aggressivity—principally among other system members (for one's own society there are already such strategies as democratization, raised incomes, etc.). At first strategies have to be introduced to ward off aggressive intentions not by the traditional method of increased armament and threat but perhaps by recourse to the findings of game theory.

(*c*) Strategies of international discussion which ensure the continual compromise model of conflict solution, without allowing blackmail.

(*d*) Strategies to correct divergent interests (e.g., in the relationship between Europe and America, or in development politics).

(*e*) Strategies to defuse manifest crises (but not crisis-management) and for transfer to less acute circumstances in which conflict-solving strategies can be applied. A further development of the U.N. peace-keeping concept is conceivable in this respect.

*   *   *

Conflict-solving strategies can be summarized as the need to achieve an effective array of instruments for peaceful change and for non-violent, or at least increasingly non-violent, further development. This requirement expresses a new notion of external policy behaviour and a demand for attention to tension-productive factors at all levels. The goal of peace research is to elucidate the foundation of conflicts and to mobilize, or at least make easier, an understanding of them, so that conflicts can be solved non-violently and equally, not with the intention of eliminating or weakening an opponent, but with co-operation as the aim. The overall goal of peace research is nothing less than to help bring about the Copernican revolution in international behaviour and in human group behaviour that will ensure some chance of human survival, but without a sacrifice of social progress and emancipation.

Naturally peace research will not take effect of itself. So that it does not remain an "academic" pursuit, every effort must be made to make its findings accessible to public opinion, politics, the educational system and individual social groups. Practices and strategies which require new forms of communication between science and politics, science and the public, and science and the educational system, form part of peace research and should not be cooped up in the ivory tower of élitist scholarship. This is an urgent task; here we can do no more than insist on its urgency.

Translated by Verdant Green